DATE DUE

AP 9'91			
17 libs			
6 √ outs to 11/07			
37 bks all this bk			

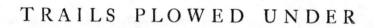

TRAILS PLOWED UNDER

TRAILS PLOWED UNDER

By CHARLES M. RUSSELL

WITH ILLUSTRATIONS IN COLOR AND LINE
BY THE AUTHOR

DOUBLEDAY

NEW YORK LONDON TORONTO SYDNEY AUCKLAND

PUBLISHED BY DOUBLEDAY

a division of Bantam Doubleday Dell Publishing Group, Inc.
666 Fifth Avenue, New York, New York 10103

DOUBLEDAY and the portrayal of an anchor with a dolphin
are trademarks of Doubleday, a division of Bantam Doubleday
Dell Publishing Group, Inc.

ISBN 0-385-04494-1

CONTENTS

OLD WEST

MAVERICKS AND STRAYS

WIDE RANGES

LIST OF COLOR ILLUSTRATIONS

LIST OF HALF-TONE ILLUSTRATIONS

LIST OF TEXT ILLUSTRATIONS

INTRODUCTION

By WILL ROGERS

The Old World.
   1926.

Hello Charley old hand, How are you?

I just thought I would drop you a line and tell you how things are a working on the old range since you left. Old Timer you don't know how we miss you, Gee but its been lonesome since you left, even to us away down here in California, where we dident get to see near as much of you as we wanted to anyhow. But think what all them old Montana Waddies are thinking. Why some of these old Birds would miss their wives less than they do you.

Nancy come down to California this fall as usual her and Jack, I dident want to tell her so and she tried to let on they wasent but I tell you they was a pretty sad looking outfit. They sho was a lonesome layout. Nancy and I talked over the usual old routine about "it all being for the best, and that you had a better job, and would do maby better work there than you did here," Yes we both said that we kinder agreed in our talk with each other, and we joshed it off and sorter smiled a little, but I want to tell you that it was a mighty sickly little grin, and between you and me, in our own hearts we knew we were both trying to load each other, We knew in each others own hearts that we couldent see why you had to go and switch outfits, just when you had got to be Boss of this one.

You know I hadent seen you in about a year, and she told me the most part of that Time, that you were working on a Book of yours even more than on your Paintings, She said you had the thing all just finished up. She said she wanted me to write a sort of an introduction to the book, Said you wanted me to before you left. My Lord Charley you know I cant write any Introduction, thats for writers to do, Why a book like you got Charley that you put all your best Stories in, and spent all that time drawing, I bet a hundred wonderful pictures are with it, Why you ought to have somebody turn an introduction out of the "schute" that would really turn on some high grade words, and doctor them up with some pretty salty ideas. It ought to be sorter classy, I couldent try to make it funny in the introduction, for you know yourself Charley what chance I got being in the same book with my little maverick brand along side of your outfit of humor. Why you never heard me open my mouth when you was around, and you never knew any of our friends that would let me open it as long as there was a chance to get you to tell another one. I always did say that you could tell a story better than any man that ever lived. If I could a got you to quit that crazy painting idea, and took up something worth while like joke telling, Why I would a set you out there on the stage at the tail end of an old chuck wagon, hunched up on an old roll of "Sougans" and a "prop" campfire burning in your face, Say you would have been the biggest thing that ever fit in while the "Glorified Beauties" was changing their color of powder. But you would dab around with them old brushes, and squeeze a handful of mud into the shape of some old "limber neck" bronk, You looked to me at times like you would ruther be a good dirt dobber, or a sort of an old painter than just about anything.

Now I am going to try to talk Nancy out of that introduction Gag to that book, Every one of your old friends are too anxious to get into the book, to be messing around with any introduction anyway, I dont know why it is but everyone of them feel that this book will be more like you than anything you have done. We can just set

there by the hour and imagine you telling that very yarn, and then
we can look at the drawing and you will show us in it the things that
we might never get if it wasent for you pointing it out to us, I bet
we get many a laugh out of all those comical drawings. I want to
see old Ed Borein when he starts a pointing out all the little cute
things in the pictures that he thinks we dont get. Some of them
stories of yours is going to be mighty sad when somebody else tries
to tell em like you did. They say your range is up on a high Mountain and you can look down on all these little outfits like ours, You
will get many a quiet laugh hearing modern "grangers" trying to
unload one of your old favorites.

There aint much news here to tell you, You know the big Boss
gent sent a hand over and got you so quick Charley, But I guess He
needed a good man pretty bad, I hear they been a working short-
handed over there pretty much all the time, I guess its hard for
Him to get hold of good men, they are just getting scarce everywhere. But you was gone one morning before the old cook could roll
out, and when you beat him up you are stepping, But after we had
realized that you had rolled your Bed and gone, it sure would a done
your old hide good to a seen what they all thought of you, You
know how it is yourself with a fellow leaving an outfit and going
over to another, in talking it over after he has gone there is generally
a BUT to it somewhere, Some old "Peeler" will unload some dirt
about him, But there sure wasent any after you crossed the skyline,
Why it would a been almost worth your going to a new Outfit just
to have heard all the fine things said about you. Why even a lot of
them old Reprobates (that perhaps owed you money) they said
"we may have Painters in time to come, that will be just as good
as old Charley, We may have Cowboys just as good, and we may
occasionally round up a pretty good man, But us, and the manicured
tribe that is following us, will never have the Real Cowboy, Painter
and Man, combined that old Charley was, For we aint got no more

real cowboys, and we aint got no real Cows to paint, and we just dont raise no more of his kind of men, and if by a Miracle we did get all that combination why it just wouldent be Charley."

Why you old Rascal you would a thought you was somebody. Why the Governor and the State Legislature of that big old commonwealth of Montana, said you was the biggest thing ever produced in the State, That your work would live and be known when maby Montana was the central part of Japan. Why we got ahold of Editorials by big Writers and Art Guys from all over the east, that said that you was the Michael Angelo of the west, (Thats some Dago over there that was as big in his day as Mussolini is now), You never was much for swelling up, but I tell you your old hat band would be busted if you had heard what was said about you.

Ah! but it was wonderful Charley, and it did please your old friends that the world recognized you. But somehow that dident seem to repay us, It wasent what you had done, it wasent because you paint a horse and a cow and a cowboy better than any man that ever lived, I dont know, it was just you Charley, We want you here if you couldent whitewash a fence, We are just sorter selfish I guess, Why when you left there was actually old "Rounders" cried, that you would a bet your last sack of tobacco that dident have any more sentiment than a wet saddle blanket. Why even your old horse followed you off with your saddle on, if you had looked back you would a seen him.

But we all know you are getting along fine, You will get along fine anywhere, I bet you hadent been up there three days till you had out your old Pencial and was a drawing something funny about some of their old punchers. That makes us want to see you more than ever for we knaow that you will have some new ones for us about some of them Sky Line Riders up there. I bet you Mark Twain and Old Bill Nye, and Whitcomb Riley and a whole bunch of those old Joshers was just a waiting for you to pop in with all the latest ones, What kind of a Bird is Washington and Jefferson I bet they are regula fellows when you meet em aint they?, most big men are. I would like to see the bunch that is gathered around you the first time you tell the one about putting the Limburger Cheese in the old Nestors Whiskers, Dont tell that Charley till you get Lincoln around you, he would love that, I bet you and him kinder throw in togeather when you get well acquainted, Darn it when I get to thinking about all them Top Hands up there, If I could just hold a Horse wrangling job with em, I wouldent mind following that wagon myself.

Write me about Bret Harte, and O Henry, I bet there is a couple of Guys standing guard togeather, auger awhile with them, and you will get many a laugh.

With that sign language that you "savvy" why you can gab with any of those old "hombres" up there, Tie in to that old Napoleon some time and pick a load into him, you ought to get something pretty good from him, if it aint nothing but about war, and women.

At first we couldent understand why they moved you, but we can now, They had every kind of a great man up there, but they just dident have any great Cowboy Artist like you. Shucks! on the luck, there was only one of you and he couldent use you both places.

You will run onto my old Dad up there Charley, For he was a real Cowhand and bet he is running a wagon, and you will pop into some well kept ranch house over under some cool shady trees and you will be asked to have dinner, and it will be the best one you ever had in your life, Well, when you are a thanking the women folks, You just tell the sweet looking little old lady that you know her boy back on an outfit you used to rep for, and tell the daughters that you knew their brother, and if you see a cute looking little rascal running around there kiss him for me. Well cant write you any more Charley dam papers all wet, It must be raining in this old bunk house.

Course we are all just a hanging on here as long as we can. I dont know why we hate to go, we know its better there, Maby its because we havent done anything that will live after we are gone.

from your old friend.

WILL.

A FEW WORDS ABOUT MYSELF

(A personal introduction written by the author but a few months before his death)

The papers have been kind to me—many times more kind than true. Although I worked for many years on the range, I am not what the people think a cowboy should be. I was neither a good roper nor rider. I was a night wrangler. How good I was, I'll leave it for the people I worked for to say—there are still a few of them living. In the spring I wrangled horses, in the fall I herded beef. I worked for the big outfits and always held my job.

I have many friends among cowmen and cowpunchers. I have always been what is called a good mixer—I had friends when I had nothing else. My friends were not always within the law, but I haven't said how law-abiding I was myself. I haven't been too bad nor too good to get along with.

Life has never been too serious with me—I lived to play and I'm playing yet. Laughs and good judgment have saved me many a black eye, but I don't laugh at other's tears. I was a wild young man, but age has made me gentle. I drank, but never alone, and when I drank it was no secret. I am still friendly with drinking men.

My friends are mixed—preachers, priests, and sinners. I belong to no church, but am friendly toward and respect all of them. I have always liked horses and since I was eight years old have always owned a few.

I am old-fashioned and peculiar in my dress. I am eccentric (that is a polite way of saying you're crazy). I believe in luck and have had lots of it.

To have talent is no credit to its owner; what man can't

help he should get neither credit nor blame for—it's not his fault. I am an illustrator. There are lots better ones, but some worse. Any man that can make a living doing what he likes is lucky, and I'm that. Any time I cash in now, I win.

CHARLES M. RUSSELL.

Great Falls, Montana

OLD WEST

SPEAKIN' of cowpunchers," says Rawhide Rawlins, "I'm glad to see in the last few years that them that know the business have been writin' about 'em. It begin to look like they'd be wiped out without a history. Up to a few years ago there's mighty little known about cows and cow people. It was sure amusin' to read some of them old stories about cowpunchin'. You'd think a puncher growed horns an' was haired over.

"It put me in mind of the eastern girl that asks her mother: 'Ma,' says she, 'do cowboys eat grass?' 'No, dear,' says the old lady, 'they're part human,' an' I don't know but the old gal had 'em sized up right. If they are human, they're a separate species. I'm talkin' about the old-time ones, before the country's strung with wire an' nesters had grabbed all the water, an' a cowpuncher's home was big. It wasn't where he took his hat off, but where he spread his blankets. He ranged from Mexico to the Big Bow River of the north, an' from where the trees get scarce in the east to the old Pacific. He don't need no iron hoss, but covers his country on one that eats grass an' wears hair. All the tools he needed was saddle, bridle, quirt, hackamore, an' rawhide riatta or seagrass rope; that covered his hoss.

"The puncher himself was rigged, startin' at the top, with a good hat—not one of the floppy kind you see in pictures, with the rim turned up in front. The top-cover he wears holds its shape an' was made to protect his face from the weather; maybe to hold it on,

I

he wore a buckskin string under the chin or back of the head. Round his neck a big silk handkerchief, tied loose, an' in the drag of a trail herd it was drawn over the face to the eyes, hold-up fashion, to protect the nose an' throat from dust. In old times, a leather blab or mask was used the same. Coat, vest, an' shirt suits his own taste. Maybe he'd wear California pants, light buckskin in color, with large brown plaid, sometimes foxed, or what you'd call reinforced with buck or antelope skin. Over these came his chaparejos or leggin's. His feet were covered with good high-heeled boots, finished off with steel spurs of Spanish pattern. His weapon's usually a forty-five Colt's six-gun, which is packed in a belt, swingin' a little below his right hip. Sometimes a Winchester in a scabbard, slung to his saddle under his stirrup-leather, either right or left side, but generally left, stock forward, lock down, as his rope hangs at his saddle-fork on the right.

"By all I can find out from old, gray-headed punchers, the cow business started in California, an' the Spaniards were the first to burn marks on their cattle an' hosses, an' use the rope. Then men from the States drifted west to Texas, pickin' up the brandin' iron an' lass-rope, an' the business spread north, east, an' west, till the spotted long-horns walked in every trail marked out by their brown cousins, the buffalo.

"Texas an' California, bein' the startin' places, made two species of cowpunchers; those west of the Rockies rangin' north, usin' centerfire or single-cinch saddles, with high fork an' cantle; packed a sixty or sixty-five foot rawhide rope, an' swung a big loop. These cow people were generally strong on pretty, usin' plenty of hoss jewelry, silver-mounted spurs, bits, an' conchas; instead of a quirt, used a romal, or quirt braided to the end of the reins. Their saddles were full stamped, with from twenty-four to twenty-eight-inch eagle-bill tapaderos. Their chaparejos were made of fur or hair, either bear, angora goat, or hair sealskin. These fellows were sure fancy, an' called themselves buccaroos, coming from the Spanish word, *vaquero*.

"The cowpuncher east of the Rockies originated in Texas and ranged north to the Big Bow. He wasn't so much for pretty; his saddle was low horn, rimfire, or double-cinch; sometimes 'macheer.' Their rope was seldom over forty feet, for being a good deal in a brush country, they were forced to swing a small loop. These men generally tied, instead of taking their dallie-welts, or wrapping their rope around the saddle horn. Their chaparejos were made of heavy bullhide, to protect the leg from brush an' thorns, with hog-snout tapaderos.

"Cowpunchers were mighty particular about their rig, an in all the camps you'd find a fashion leader. From a cowpuncher's idea, these fellers was sure good to look at, an' I tell you right now, there ain't no prettier sight for my eyes than one of those good-lookin', long-backed cowpunchers, sittin' up on a high-forked, full-stamped California saddle with a live hoss between his legs.

"Of course a good many of these fancy men were more orna-mental than useful, but one of the best cow-hands I ever knew be-longed to this class. Down on the Gray Bull, he went under the name of Mason, but most punchers called him Pretty Shadow. This sounds like an Injun name, but it ain't. It comes from a habit some punchers has of ridin' along, lookin' at their shadows. Lookin' glasses are scarce in cow outfits, so the only chance for these pretty boys to admire themselves is on bright, sunshiny days. Mason's one of these kind that doesn't get much pleasure out of life in cloudy weather. His hat was the best; his boots was made to order, with extra long heels. He rode a center-fire, full-stamped saddle, with twenty-eight-inch tapaderos; bearskin ancaroes, or saddle pockets; his chaparejos were of the same skin. He packed a sixty-five-foot rawhide. His spurs an' bit were silver inlaid, the last bein' a Span-ish spade. But the gaudiest part of his regalia was his gun. It's a

A CENTER-FIRE FASHION LEADER

forty-five Colt's, silverplated an' chased with gold. Her handle is
pearl, with a bull's head carved on.

"When the sun hits Mason with all this silver on, he blazes
up like some big piece of jewelry. You could see him for miles when
he's ridin' high country. Barrin' Mexicans, he's the fanciest cow dog
I ever see, an' don't think he don't savvy the cow. He knows what
she says to her calf. Of course there wasn't many of his stripe. All
punchers liked good rigs, but plainer; an' as most punchers 're
fond of gamblin' an' spend their spare time at stud poker or monte,
they can't tell what kind of a rig they'll be ridin' the next day. I've
seen many a good rig lost over a blanket. It depends how lucky the
cards fall what kind of a rig a man's ridin'.

"I'm talkin' about old times, when cowmen were in their
glory. They lived different, talked different, an' had different ways.
No matter where you met him, or how he's rigged, if you'd watch
him close he'd do something that would tip his hand. I had a little
experience back in '83 that'll show what I'm gettin' at.

"I was winterin' in Cheyenne. One night a stranger stakes me
to buck the bank. I got off lucky an' cash in fifteen hundred dollars.
Of course I cut the money in two with my friend, but it leaves me
with the biggest roll I ever packed. All this wealth makes Cheyenne
look small, an' I begin longin' for bigger camps, so I drift for
Chicago. The minute I hit the burg, I shed my cow garments an'
get into white man's harness. A hard hat, boiled shirt, laced shoes—
all the gearin' known to civilized man. When I put on all this rig,
I sure look human; that is, I think so. But them shorthorns know
me, an' by the way they trim that roll, it looks like somebody 's
pinned a card on my back with the word 'EASY' in big letters. I
ain't been there a week till my roll don't need no string around it,
an' I start thinkin' about home. One evenin' I throw in with the
friendliest feller I ever met. It was at the bar of the hotel where I'm
camped. I don't just remember how we got acquainted, but after

about fifteen drinks we start holdin' hands an' seein' who could buy the most and fastest. I remember him tellin' the barslave not to take my money, 'cause I'm his friend. Afterwards, I find out the reason for this goodheartedness; he wants it all an' hates to see me waste it. Finally, he starts to show me the town an' says it won't cost me a cent. Maybe he did, but I was unconscious, an' wasn't in shape to remember. Next day, when I come to, my hair's sore an' I didn't know the days of the week, month, or what year it was.

"The first thing I do when I open my eyes is to look at the winders. There's no bars on 'em, an' I feel easier. I'm in a small room with two bunks. The one opposite me holds a feller that's smokin' a cigarette an' sizin' me up between whiffs while I'm dressin'. I go through myself but I'm too late. Somebody beat me to it. I'm lacin' my shoes an' thinkin' hard, when the stranger speaks:

"'Neighbor, you're a long way from your range.'

"'You call the turn,' says I, 'but how did you read my iron?'

"'I didn't see a burn on you,' says he, 'an' from looks, you'll go as a slick-ear. It's your ways, while I'm layin' here, watchin' you get into your garments. Now, humans dress up an' punchers dress down. When you raised, the first thing you put on is your hat. Another thing that shows you up is you don't shed your shirt when you bed down. So next comes your vest an' coat, keepin' your hind-quarters covered till you slide into your pants, an' now you're lacin' your shoes. I notice you done all of it without quittin' the blankets, like the ground's cold. I don't know what state or territory you hail from, but you've smelt sagebrush an' drank alkali. I heap savvy you. You've slept a whole lot with nothin' but sky over your head, an' there's times when that old roof leaks, but judgin' from appearances, you wouldn't mind a little open air right now.'

"This feller's my kind, an' he stakes me with enough to get back to the cow country."

A GIFT HORSE

CHARLEY FURIMAN tells me about a hoss he owns and if you're able to stay on him he'll take you to the end of the trail. The gent Charley got him from, says he, "Gentle? He's a pet." (This man hates to part with him.) "He's a lady's hoss. You can catch him anywhere with a biscuit."

Next day Charley finds out he's a lady's hoss, all right, but he don't like men. Furiman ain't a mile from his corral when he slips the pack. Charley crawls him again kinder careful and rides him sixty miles an' he don't turn a hair. Next day he saddles him he acts like he's harmless but he's looking for something. He's out about ten mile. Charley notices he travels with one ear down. This ain't a good sign, but Charley gets careless and about noon he comes to a dry creek bed where there's lots of boulders. That's what this cayuse is looking for 'cause right in the middle of the boulder-strewn flat is where he breaks in two and unloads. Charley tells me, "I don't miss none of them boulders an' where I light there's nothing gives but different parts of me. For a while I wonder where I'm at and when things do clear up it comes to me right quick. I forgot to bring the biscuits. How am I going to catch him? If I had a Winchester, I'd catch him just over the eye.

"To make a long story short, I followed him back to the ranch afoot. Walking ain't my strong holt an' these boulder bumps don't help me none. Next morning after a good night's sleep, I feel better. Going out to the corral, I offer this cayuse a biscuit, thinkin' I'll start off friendly. He strikes at me and knocks my hat off. My pardner tries to square it by telling me I ain't got the right kind. 'That's a lady's hoss,' says he, 'and being a pet, he wants them

7

little lady's biscuits; it's enough to make him sore, handing him them sour doughs.'

"While I'm getting my hat, I happen to think of a friend of mine that's got married and I ain't give him no wedding present. This friend of mine is a bronk rider named Con Price. So while my heart's good, I saddle a gentle hoss and lead this man-hater over and presents him to Price with my best wishes.

"I don't meet Con till next fall on the beef roundup. He ain't too friendly. Next morning when we're roping hosses, he steps up to me and says, kinder low, holdin' out his hand to shake, 'Charley, I'm letting bygones be bygones, but if I get married again anywhere in your neighborhood, don't give me no wedding presents. If you do you'll get lots of flowers.'"

"HE UNLOADS ME RIGHT IN THE MIDDLE OF THE
BOULDER-STREWN FLAT"

TALKIN' about Christmas," said Bedrock, as we smoked in his cabin after supper, an' the wind howled as it sometimes can on a blizzardy December night, "puts me in mind of one I spent in the '60s. Me an' a feller named Jake Mason, but better knowed as Beaver, is trappin' an' prospectin' on the head of the Porcupine. We've struck some placer, but she's too cold to work her. The snow's drove all the game out of the country, an' barrin' a few beans and some flour, we're plum out of grub, so we decide we'd better pull our freight before we're snowed in.

"The winter's been pretty open till then, but the day we start there's a storm breaks loose that skins everything I ever seed. It looks like the snow-maker's been holdin' back, an' turned the whole winter supply loose at once. Cold? Well, it would make a polar bear hunt cover.

"About noon it lets up enough so we can see our pack-hosses. We're joggin' along at a good gait, when old Baldy, our lead pack-hoss, stops an' swings 'round in the trail, bringin' the other three to a stand. His whinner causes me to raise my head, an' lookin' under my hat brim, I'm plenty surprised to see an old log shack not ten feet to the side of the trail.

"'I guess we'd better take that cayuse's advice,' says Beaver, pintin' to Baldy, who's got his ears straightened, lookin' at us as much as to say: 'What, am I packin' fer Pilgrims; or don't you know enough to get in out of the weather? It looks like you'd loosen these packs.' So, takin' Baldy's hunch, we unsaddle.

"This cabin's mighty ancient. It's been two rooms, but the ridge-pole on the rear one's rotted an' let the roof down. The door's

9

wide open an' hangs on a wooden hinge. The animal smell I get on the inside tells me there ain't no humans lived there for many's the winter. The floor's strewn with pine cones an' a few scattered bones, showin' it's been the home of mountain-rats an' squirrels. Takin' it all 'n all, it ain't no palace, but, in this storm, it looks mighty snug, an' when we get a blaze started in the fireplace an' the beans goin' it's comfortable.

"The door to the back's open, an' by the light of the fire I can see the roof hangin' down V-shaped, leavin' quite a little space

'I'M PLENTY SURPRISED TO SEE AN OLD LOG SHACK TO THE
SIDE OF THE TRAIL'

agin the wall. Once I had a notion of walkin' in an' prospectin' the place, but there's somethin' ghostly about it an' I change my mind.

"When we're rollin' in that night, Beaver asks me what day of the month it is.

"'If I'm right on my dates,' says I, 'this is the evenin' the kids hang up their socks.'

"'The hell it is,' says he. 'Well, here's one camp Santy'll prob-ably overlook. We ain't got no socks nor no place to hang 'em, an' I don't think the old boy'd savvy our foot-rags.' That's the last I remember till I'm waked up along in the night by somethin' mon-keyin' with the kettle.

"If it wasn't fer a snufflin' noise I could hear, I'd a-tuk it fer a trade-rat, but with this noise it's no guess with me, an' I call the turn all right, 'cause when I take a peek, there, humped be-tween me an' the fire, is the most robust silvertip I ever see. In size, he resembles a load of hay. The fire's down low, but there's enough light to give me his outline. He's humped over, busy with the beans, snifflin' an' whinin' pleasant, like he enjoys 'em. I nudged Beaver easy, an' whispers: 'Santy Claus is here.'

"He don't need but one look. 'Yes,' says he, reachin' for his Henry, 'but he ain't brought nothin' but trouble, an' more'n a sock full of that. You couldn't crowd it into a wagon-box.'

"This whisperin' disturbs Mr. Bear, an' he straightens up till he near touches the ridge-pole. He looks eight feet tall. Am I scared? Well, I'd tell a man. By the feelin' runnin' up and down my back, if I had bristles I'd resemble a wild hog. The cold sweat's drippin' off my nose, an' I ain't got nothin' on me but sluice-ice.

"The bark of Beaver's Henry brings me out of this scare. The bear goes over, upsettin' a kettle of water, puttin' the fire out. If it wasn't for a stream of fire runnin' from Beaver's weapon, we'd be in plumb darkness. The bear's up agin, bellerin' an' bawlin', and comin' at us mighty warlike, and by the time I get my Sharp's workin', I'm near choked with smoke. It's the noisiest muss I was ever mixed up in. Between the smoke, the barkin' of the guns an' the bellerin' of the bear, it's like hell on a holiday.

"I'm gropin' for another ca'tridge when I hear the lock on

Beaver's gun click, an' I know his magazine's dry. Lowerin' my hot gun, I listen. Everythin's quiet now. In the sudden stillness I can hear the drippin' of blood. It's the bear's life runnin' out.

"'I guess it's all over,' says Beaver, kind of shaky. 'It was a short fight, but a fast one, an' hell was poppin' while she lasted.'

"When we get the fire lit, we take a look at the battle ground.

"THE BEAR'S COMIN' AT US MIGHTY WARLIKE"

There lays Mr. Bear in a ring of blood, with a hide so full of holes he wouldn't hold hay. I don't think there's a bullet went 'round him.

"This excitement wakens us so we don't sleep no more that night. We breakfast on bear meat. He's an old bear an' it's pretty stout, but a feller livin' on beans and bannocks straight for a couple of weeks don't kick much on flavor, an' we're at a stage where meat's meat.

"When it comes day, me an' Beaver goes lookin' over the bear's bedroom. You know, daylight drives away ha'nts, an' this room don't look near so ghostly as it did last night. After winnin' this fight, we're both mighty brave. The roof caved in with four or five feet of snow on, makes the rear room still dark, so, lightin' a pitch-pine glow, we start explorin'.

"The first thing we bump into is the bear's bunk. There's a rusty pick layin' up against the wall, an' a gold-pan on the floor, showin' us that the human that lived there was a miner. On the other side of the shack we ran onto a pole bunk, with a weather-wrinkled buffalo robe an' some rotten blankets. The way the roof slants, we can't see into the bed, but by usin' an axe an' choppin' the legs off, we lower it to view. When Beaver raises the light, there's the frame-work of a man. He's layin' on his left side, like he's sleepin', an' looks like he cashed in easy. Across the bunk, under his head, is an old-fashioned cap-'n-ball rifle. On the bedpost hangs a powder horn an' pouch, with a belt an' skinnin' knife. These things tell us that this man's a pretty old-timer.

"Findin' the pick an' gold-pan causes us to look more careful for what he'd been diggin'. We explore the bunk from top to bottom, but nary a find. All day long we prospects. That evenin', when we're fillin' up on bear meat, beans and bannocks, Beaver says he's goin' to go through the bear's bunk; so, after we smoke, relightin' our torches, we start our search again.

"Sizin' up the bear's nest, we see he'd laid there quite a while. It looks like Mr. Silvertip, when the weather gets cold, starts huntin' a winter location for his long snooze. Runnin' onto this cabin, vacant, and lookin' like it's for rent, he jumps the claim an' would have been snoozin' there yet, but our fire warmin' up the place fools him. He thinks it's spring an' steps out to look at the weather. On the way he strikes this breakfast of beans, an' they hold him till we object.

"We're lookin' over this nest when somethin' catches my eye on the edge of the waller. It's a hole, roofed over with willers.

"'Well, I'll be damned. There's his cache,' says Beaver, whose eyes has follered mine. It don't take a minute to kick these willers loose, an' there lays a buckskin sack with five hundred dollars in dust in it.

"'Old Santy Claus, out there,' says Beaver, pointin' to the bear through the door, 'didn't load our socks, but he brought plenty of meat an' showed us the cache, for we'd never a-found it if he hadn't raised the lid.'

"The day after Christmas we buried the bones, wrapped in one of our blankets, where we'd found the cache. It was the best we could do.

"'I guess the dust's ours,' says Beaver. 'There's no papers to show who's his kin-folks.' So we splits the pile an' leaves him sleepin' in the tomb he built for himself."

D UNC McDONALD, the breed, tells about a buffalo hunt
he has when he's a kid," says Rawhide Rawlins. "Like
all things that happen that's worth while, it's a long time
ago. He's traveling with his people, the Blackfeet—they're making
for the buffalo country. They're across the range—they ain't seen
much maybe—an old bull once in a while that ain't worth shootin'
at, so they don't disturb nothin'. They're lookin' for cow meat
and lots of it.

"Dunc's traveling ahead of the women with the men. As I
said, it's a long time ago when Injuns ain't got many guns—they're
mostly armed with bows and arrows. There's one old man packing
a rifle. It's a Hudson Bay flintlock but a good gun, them days.
Duncan is young and has good eyes that go with youth. He sees
a few buffalo in some broken hills, and tells this old man if he'll
lend him his gun, he'll get meat. The old man don't say nothin',
but taking the gun from its skin cover, hands it to Dunc. Dunc
wants bullets and the powder horn but the old man signs that the
gun is loaded, and one ball is enough for any good hunter. The
wolf hunts with what teeth he's got.

"Dunc knows he won't get no more so he rides off. There
ain't much wind, but Dunc's gettin' what there is, and keepin'
behind some rock croppin's he gets pretty close. There are five
cows, all laying down. Pretty soon he quits his pony and crawls to
within twenty-five yards and pulls down a fat cow. When his gun
roars, they all jump and run but the cow he shoots don't make
three jumps till she's down.

"When Dunc walks up she's laying on her belly with her feet

under her. She's small but fat. When Dunc puts his foot agin her to push her over, she gets up and is red-eyed. She sure shows war. The only hold Dunc can see is her tail and he ain't slow takin' it. The tail-hold on a buffalo is mighty short, but he's clamped on. She's tryin' to turn but he's keepin' her steered right—and he's doing fine till she starts kickin'. The first one don't miss his ear the width of a hair. If you never saw a buffalo kick it's hard to tell you what they can do, but Dunc ain't slow slippin' his hold.

"There's nothin' left but to run for it. This rock croppin' ain't over two feet high, but it's all there is. These rocks are covered with ground cedar and Dunc dives into this. He gophers down in this cedar till a hawk couldn't find him. He lays there a long time, his heart poundin' his ribs like it will break through. When the scare works out of him he raises, and there agin the rock rim lays the cow—it's a lung shot and she's bled to death.

"'There's only one hold,' says Dunc, 'shorter than a tail-hold on a buffalo—that of a bear.'"

"A TAIL-HOLD ON A BUFFALO"

I'M GETTIN' mighty weary of holin' up in this line camp," said Long Wilson, scratching the frost from the window and gazing discontentedly out at the storm. "If the snow ever lets up, it'll be fine trackin' weather, an' chances 'll be good for a blacktail over on Painted Ridge."

"Tracks 'd do you a whole lot of good, old scout," said Bowlegs, sitting up cross-legged in the bunk and rolling a cigarette. "You couldn't track a bed-wagon through a boghole. I ain't forgot last winter, when you're lost on Dog Creek. You're ridin' in a circle, follerin' your own trail, an' you'd a-been there yet if the Cross H boys hadn't found you. You're a tracker, I don't think."

"Speakin' of trackin'," broke in Dad Lane, the wolfer, "reminds me of a cripple I knowed who goes by the name of Reel Foot. He's one of nature's mistakes, a born deformity. It looks like when Old Lady Nature built him, she starts from the top an' does good work till she gets to his middle, an' then throws off the job to somebody that's workin' for fun.

"This cripple was before your time, but he's well known on the lower Yellerstone in the early '70s. The first winter I ever see Reel Foot I'm sittin' in a poker game with him. Now, lookin' at him across the table, he'll average up with any man for shape an' looks, but at this time I ain't acquainted with him from his waist down.

"For two weeks I've been eatin' plenty booze, an' I'm at that stage where I see things that ain't there. Old Four-Ace Jack that's handin' us the beverage, looks like twins; my sight's doublin' up on me. The game's goin' along smooth enough till I reach for a pot on a pair of aces, an' Reel Foot claims I only got one. There's quite a little argument, an' while he's convincin' me I spill some chips. When I'm gropin' 'round for 'em under the table, I run onto them hoofs, warped an' twisted. As I said before, I ain't acquainted with his hind quarters, an' it rattles me till I see feet enough for four men, an' there's only two of us playin'. This ends the game with me, so cashin' in, I tell Four-Ace to pour my drink back in the bottle. I'm that shaky I couldn't empty it into a barrel with the head out, an' don't swallow no more booze that trip.

"The scare wears off when I get acquainted with Reel Foot, but I never do look at him without wonderin' which way he's goin' to start off. His right foot's straight ahead, natural; the left, p'intin' back on his trail. It's an old sayin', 'a fool for luck,' an' in this case, I guess it goes with cripples, for it's these twisted hin' legs of his'n that saves his hide an' hair for him once.

"It happens when he first hits the country from Nebrasky. He's camped on the Porcupine, an' as trappin's good an' he's figurin' on staying awhile, he's throwed up a lean-to of brush. He's one of these kind that don't get lonesome, an' 'lows if you don't mix with no worse company than animals you're all right. Livin' so long with cayuses, he savvies 'em an' they understand him. They even seem to know what he's talkin' to 'em about.

"One mornin' Reel Foot leaves camp to visit his traps. He's on his pony, but about a mile down the creek, the brush bein' thick, he quits the cayuse an' goes afoot. After visitin' his traps Reel Foot circles 'round an' doubles back on his old trail a couple of hundred yards below where his hoss is tied. When he reaches his cayuse he climbs on an' rides into camp.

"Now, there's a bunch of Ogallaly Sioux in this country, led by Blood Lance. They're runnin' buffalo, an' one day they find where some whites has made a killin' an' tuk nothin' but the tongues This waste of meat makes their hearts bad, an' it wouldn't be healthy for no whites they run across. Their feelin's are stirred up this way when they strike Reel Foot's tracks, which causes them to pull up their ponies, an' every Injun skins his gun. There's snow on the ground, so the readin's plain. He's wearin' moccasins, but that don't fool 'em none; they see where he's shuk out his pipe while he's walkin'. This tells 'em he's a white man, 'cause Injuns don't smoke while they're travelin'. Whenever a redskin lights his pipe, you can bet he's down on his hunkers, takin' comfort.

"'My brothers,' says one wise old buck who's been sittin' wrapped in his blanket, sayin' nothin', 'are the Ogallalys like the bat that cannot see in the light of the sun? Shall we sit an' talk like women while these men with hair on their faces, who leave our meat to rot on the prairie, walk from under our knives an' laugh at us? I am old an' do not boast of the eye of the hawk, but it's as plain as the travois tracks in the snow; there are two men.'

"After studyin' the tracks awhile they decide the old man's right. There are two one-legged men travelin' in opposite direc-tions. From the length of the strides showed by the tracks, they figger these men are long in the leg, an' must be very tall. They talk it over an' decide to split the party an' take both trails.

"Of course, they go lookin' for the track of a crutch or wooden leg, but finally the only way they can figger it out is that these two men's travelin' by hoppin', an' the tricks these cripples does has them savages guessin'. There's one place where Reel Foot's jumped off a cutbank; it's anyway ten feet straight down. Now for the cripple that jumps down, it is easy, but what's worryin' these Injuns is how the other one-legged man stands flat-footed an' bounds up the bank, lightin' easy, with no sign of scramblin'.

"When the party that takes the trail towards camp gets to where Reel Foot doubles back, they're plenty puzzled. Injun-like, these fellers are superstitious, an' when the tracks run together, they're gettin' scary.

"'It looks like the tracks of two two-legged men walkin' in

opposite directions,' says a young buck named Weasel. 'Or else the one-legged men have found their lost legs.'

"But the old wise man says: 'Again the young buck has the eyes of the bat. There are four tracks; two of the right foot an' two of the left. These are the tracks of four one-legged men.'

"THEY DECIDE THERE'S TWO ONE-LEGGED MEN TRAVELIN'
IN OPPOSITE DIRECTIONS"

"Some thinks it's the work of ghosts an' are willin' to turn back, but their curiosity downs their fear, an' they foller the trail mighty shaky till they run onto where Reel Foot mounts his hoss. Here they figger that two of these one-legged men got off the hoss, while the other two, comin' the opposite way, get on an' ride into the willers.

"By this time these savages are so rattled that the snappin' of a twig would turn the whole band back. They're beginnin' to think they've struck the land of one-legged men, an' they're follerin' the trail mighty cautious when they sight the smoke of Reel Foot's camp.

"Now when the Reel Foot gets in from his traps, he's mighty leg-weary after draggin' them warped feet of his'n through the snow. So the minute he gets some grub under his belt, he freshens the fire an' beds down with his feet stickin' out towards the warmth. He's layin' this way asleep, when these killers come up on him. The minute they sight his feet, every buck's hand goes to his mouth, an' when an Injun does this, he's plenty astonished. All the tricks in the tracks are plain to 'em now. Some of 'em are hostile an' are for killin' him, but the old men of the party say it is not good to kill a man whose tracks have fooled the hawk-eyed Ogallalys. Deformities amongst these people are few an' far between. In buildin' all wild animals Nature makes few mistakes, Injuns 're only part human, an' when you see a cripple among 'em, it's safe bettin' that somebody's worked him over.

"They don't even wake Reel Foot, but coverin' their guns an' crawlin' their ponies, sneak away. When he raises from his nap he finds pony an' moccasin tracks, but never knows how close he comes to crossin' the range till about two years later, me an' him's in a Ogallaly camp doin' some tradin'. We're in Blood Lance's lodge, smokin' an' dickerin' on this swap, when Blood Lance, who's been starin' at Reel Foot between puffs, lays down the pipe an' signs he knows him. 'Those feet,' says he, pointin' to Reel Foot's twisted legs, 'fooled the Ogallalys an' saved the white man's hair,' an' with that he spins us the yarn of Reel Foot's crooked tracks. Always after, he's knowed amongst the Ogallalys as 'The Man-Who-Walks-Both-Ways.'"

"THE OLD CAYUSE STARTS TRYIN' TO OUT-DODGE THESE WOLVES"

22

BULLARD'S WOLVES

LOTS of cowpunchers like to play with a rope, but ropes, like guns, are dangerous. All the difference is, guns go off and ropes go on. So you'll savvy my meanin', I'll tell you a story.

One time Bill Bullard's jogging along towards camp when he bumps into a couple of wolves that's been agin a bait. They've got enough strychnine so they're stiff and staggerin'. Bill drops his loop on one easy. Then he thinks, "What's the matter with taking both?" So he puts a couple of half hitches in the middle of his string, drops 'em over the horn, builds a loop at the other end of his rope, and dabs it on the second wolf. He's snaking 'em along all right till one of these calf-killers bumps on a sagebrush and bounces too near his hoss.

Right then's when the ball opens. The old hoss will stand anything but he don't like the smell of these meat eaters, so when this one starts crowdin' him, snappin' his teeth, he goes hog-wild; and wherever he's goin' Bill don't know, but the gait he takes it's a cinch they won't be late. Tain't so bad till they hit the sagebrush country. Then, first one and then another bounces by Bill's head and lands ahead of him. This old cayuse starts trying to out-dodge this couple. Mr. Bullard manages to keep his cayuse headed for the camp, but he's mighty busy staying in the middle of this living lightning he's riding.

When the boys in camp see him coming down the bottom, they all wonder what's his hurry, but they heap savvy when they see what's following him. He don't slow up none when he reaches camp, so the boys hand him some remarks like: "What's your hurry, Bill, won't you stay to eat?" "Don't hurry, Bill, you got lots of time." "If you're going to Medicine Hat, a little more to the left!"

Bullard's red-eyed by this time, and of course these remarks cheer him up a whole lot. A little more and Bill would bite himself. If he had a gun, there'd be a massacre. Finally the hoss wrangler, who's afraid Bill will mix with the saddle band, rides out and herds the whole muss into the rope corral.

When Bullard dismounts he don't say nothing an' it don't look safe to ask questions.

Bill's mighty quiet for days. About a week later somebody says something about killin' two birds with one stone. "Yes," says Bill, "maybe you'll kill two birds with one stone but don't ever bet you can get two anythings with one rope."

SOME of these wise book-learned men claim that our red brothers come from China but they can't prove it," says Murphy. "These folks ain't got no history, barring a few paintin's or carvin's on rocks. They don't write—these folks ain't got no books, an' books are back-tracks of man. An Injun can't tell you further back than his grand-dad told him, an' you can't back-track far on grass and most Injun trails are grass-grown.

"If I told only what I know about Injuns, I'd be through right now. I run on to a beaver house last fall. It looked the same as the first one I ever saw—that's over forty-five years ago. The Injun is no different—the buffalo skin lodge of long ago is the same thing as the canvas lodge of to-day. What changes the red man has made, he took from his white brothers.

"The big change came when old Cortez brought that three-cross brand of hosses over. Mr. Injun wasn't long afoot. Before this he had only wolves broke to pack or drag a travois. The country was lousy with meat but in open spaces it ain't easy to get when you're afoot. The Injuns, like their brother, the wolf, followed the herds. The wolf had the edge with his four legs, and when the wolf made his kill it's a safe bet that if there was enough Injuns so they wouldn't be bashful, they took it away from Mr. Wolf and sometimes they took what the wolf left. When man gets his feed this way, he don't get his meals often or regular enough to hurt his digestion, an' where meat lays too long in hot weather, it doesn't need cooking—but when you go a few days without eatin', you won't mind this.

"Sometimes they'd run buffalo off cliffs. These were big kill-

in's. This was pulled by the medicine man who owned a buffalo
stone. I've seen one of these stones. Injuns claim this stone could
call buffalo. It's a queer-looking rock about the size of your fist.
If a band of buffalo comes near one of these cliffs, Mr. Medicine
Man goes out with his stone. He ain't wearing much but his robe.
Under that he's stripped, knowing, if he's lucky, he's got to make a
race out of it and outrun the buffalo. He gets as near as he can
to the herd, wraps his robe around him and gets down on his hands
and knees an' starts going through all kinds of manœuvres, makin'
noises and at the same time working towards the cliff.

"While this is going on, the rest of his folks is sneaking up
behind the buffalo that's so busy watchin' this thing that's wearing one of their hides. Naturally, the buffalo want to know what
this thing is that dresses like them, but ain't got no shape that they
ever saw. This medicine man knows enough; he's got their wind,
they can't smell him. They follow him slow first, but soon they're
running. When they're close enough to the cliff, he drops his robe,
and makes a getaway. When they try to turn, all these Injuns behind them rares up, waving their robes and yelling. In a minute
they're all millin' and crowdin' till most of them, maybe all, go
over, an' them that ain't killed are crippled so bad they're easy
finished with lances or arrows.

"I seen one of these places near the Teton River, where there's
three feet of buffalo bones, about a hundred yards long under this
cliff. Them days, the squaws stripped the meat with their knives,
leaving the bones. At this place the whites gather arrow heads to
this day. Them they find are stone, telling that it happened a long
time ago. There are layers of buffalo hair and wool that looks like
felt.

"Such places were called by the Blackfeet, *piscum*. These
places weren't used much, I don't think, after they got the hoss—
they didn't need them. With a good hoss under him, a bow and ar-

rows with steel or iron points that the white traders brought, it was easy for an Injun to get meat.

"While the buffalo lasted, the Injuns counted their wealth in hosses. The Injun always was a trouble hunter, and getting hosses don't make him any easier to get along with. Whites that don't know him think he never smiles. They got this idea walking into lodges without no invite, pickin' up anything they see. Maybe the owner of this lodge is talking to a friend. The white man thinks it's all right to stand between these two redskins. If the Injun is smoking, the civilized man takes the pipe and examines it. If there's a party of these wedge-ins, they're picking things up and talking and making all kinds of remarks—one'll tell the rest what dirty people Injuns are. Maybe there's an Injun in the lodge that savvys white man talk; if he does, he ain't slow tellin' what the white man says. Naturally, the red man that's been starving for years on white man's promises ain't got lots of love for him, so when he busts in on his home and fireside, the Injun don't show much joy. If other people would walk into my house without bein' asked, I don't think I'd smile an' look pleasant. What would

"BEFORE THIS HE ONLY HAD WOLVES BROKE TO PACK
OR DRAG A TRAVOIS"

I do if I wasn't able to throw them out? I'd call the police. An Injun laughs only when it's on the square.

"Some white men, especially these wedgers-in, are as welcome in an Injun camp as a rattlesnake in a dog town. If an Injun likes you, he'll go to the end of the trail for you; if he don't, he'll go further the other way. If he's a friend, anything he's got is yours. If he don't like you, anything you got is his if he can get away with it. Whites will do the same, I notice, in war times. We stole every inch of land we got from the Injun but we didn't get it without a fight, and Uncle Sam will remember him a long time.

"The whites have always held the edge. The first were Spaniards with steel bow-guns and with clothes made by a blacksmith. Mister Injun met him with wooden bows an' stone-pointed arrows, and paint wasn't much protection against a bow-gun that would drive an iron bolt through a steel plate. The only chance an Injun had to get a Spaniard was when he's in bathing, an' beaches were only used them days to land boats on, and folks didn't bathe often —it wasn't considered healthy, and I imagine the white man's camp was a little stronger than a wolf den if the wind's right. It's no trick for Mr. Injun to locate the camp, but what's the good? His stone arrow heads only bust on this iron shell the white man wears. When the white man gets the gun, an Injun gets one too but he ain't got no powder—he's always a few jumps behind, but by doing some careful sneakin' he gets enough scalps to trim his leggin's. Then there are so many whites that's baldheaded that it's hardly worth the Injun's while takin' chances, for when he's got so he can load a flintlock gun in twenty minutes, the paleface shows up with a britch-loader. When he gets a britch-loader, the white man's got a repeater.

"If you're out looking for a man with a repeater and you are packin' a missile stuffer and you got powder that's wet, naturally you're careful. The man with a repeater and belt full of cartridges calls the feller with a single shot a coward. Of course, this makes a bush-whacker out of an Injun.

"I believe if the white man had the same weapons as his red brothers, Uncle Sam wouldn't own only part of this country yet and we wouldn't need any game law. I think the white man is the smartest man in the world but he's no braver than others. He's the smartest, he's proved that. He's the only man in the world that plays golf to keep himself in shape—other colors keep the extry leaf-lard off with a pick and shovel. The old-time Injun didn't pack much fat. He didn't work, but he was busy finding meat and dodgin' enemies. Civilization don't agree with him—he ain't got room. A few more generations an' there won't be a full blood American left."

"THE BIG CHANGE CAME WHEN OLD CORTEZ BROUGHT HOSSES OVER"

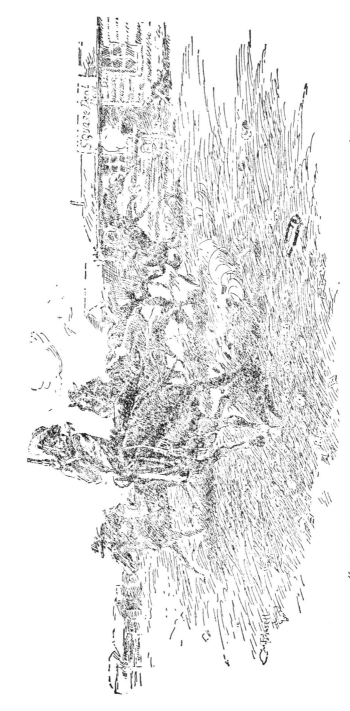

"COWPUNCHERS WERE CARELESS, HOMELESS, HARD-DRINKING MEN"

WHISKEY

WHISKEY has been blamed for lots it didn't do. It's a brave-maker. All men know it. If you want to know a man, get him drunk and he'll tip his hand. If I like a man when I'm sober, I kin hardly keep from kissing him when I'm drunk. This goes both ways. If I don't like a man when I'm sober, I don't want him in the same town when I'm drunk.

Remember, I ain't saying that booze is good for men, but it boils what's in him to the top. A man that beats his wife when he's drunk ain't a good man when he's sober. I've knowed drunks that would come home to mama loaded down with flowers, candy, and everything that they thought their wife would like. Other men that wouldn't take a drink never brought home nothing but laundry soap. The man that comes home drunk and licks his wife wouldn't fight a chickadee when he's sober. The drunk that brings home presents knows he's wrong and is sorry. He wants to square himself. The man that licks his wife ain't sorry for nobody but himself, and the only way to make him real sorry is to beat him near to death.

There's a difference in whiskey—some's worse than others. Me and a friend drops into a booze parlor on the Canadian line. The man that runs this place is a friend of ours. I ain't mentioning no names but his front name's Dick. He's an old-time cowpuncher. He's bought a lot of booze in his day but right now he's selling it.

When me and my friend name our drink we notice there's about ten men in this joint. Their actions tells us they've been using some of Dick's goods, but there ain't no loud talk. They are all paired off, talking low like they're at a funeral. I get curious and

31

ask Dick if these gents are pallbearers that's spreading sorrow on his joint.

"No," says Dick, looking wise. "This ain't no cow-town no more. It's one of the coming farmer-cities of this country, and the sellers of all this rich land don't want nothing that'll scare away farmers, and I'm here to please the folks. Most of these tillers of the soil come from prohibition states where men do their drinkin' alone in the cellar. When you drink that way, it don't cost so much. The old-timer that you knew was generally on the square. When he got drunk he wanted everybody to know it and they did, if they were in the same town. Folks to-day ain't been able to sweep all this old stuff out but, like some old bachelors I know, they've swept the dirt under the bed, and what you don't see don't look bad.

"The gent that sold me this brand of booze told me there ain't a cross word in a barrel of it, and he told the truth. All these gents you see in here are pleasant without the noise. This bunch, if they stay to the finish, will whisper themselves to sleep. This booze would be safe for a burglar. I call it," says Dick, "whisperin' booze."

But as I said before, there's different kinds. I knowed a old Injun trader on the Missouri River that sold another kind. Back in the '80s the cowmen of Judith country was throwing their cattle north of the river. This old trader had a place on the river right where we crossed the cattle. All summer we were swimming herds.

I never knowed what made an Injun so crazy when he drunk till I tried this booze. I always was water shy and this old stream has got many a man, but with a few drinks of this trade whiskey the Missouri looked like a creek and we spur off in it with no fear. It was sure a brave-maker, and if a man had enough of this booze you couldn't drown him. You could even shoot a man through the brain or heart and he wouldn't die till he sobered up.

When Injuns got their hides full of this they were bad and dangerous. I used to think this was because an Injun was a wild man, but at this place where we crossed the herds there's about ten lodges of Assiniboines, and we all get drunk together. The squaws, when we started, got mighty busy caching guns and knives. In an hour we're all, Injuns and whites, so disagreeable that a shepherd dog couldn't have got along with us. Some wise cowpuncher had persuaded all the cowpunchers to leave their guns in camp. This wise man could see ahead an' knowed things was going to be messy. Without guns either cowpunchers or Injuns are harmless—they can't do nothing but pull hair. Of course the Injun, wearing his locks long, gets the worst of it. We were so disagreeable that the Injuns had to move camp.

It used to be agin the law to sell an Injun whiskey, but the law has made Injuns out of all of us now. Most new booze is worse than trade whiskey. Whiskey made all men brave. If nobody got drunk the East Coast would be awful crowded by this time. Maybe the leaders of the exploring party didn't drink, but the men that went with them did. It's a safe bet there wasn't a man in Columbus' crew that knowed what a maple-nut sundae was.

In the old times, when the world had lots of wild countries and some brave explorer wanted men to go up agin danger and maybe starvation, he don't go to the fireside of home lovers; he finds the toughest street in a town where there's music, booze, and lots of fighters—he ain't lookin' for pets. When he steps in this joint, he walks to the bar and asks them all up. He don't bar nobody, not even the bartender. He starts with making a good feller of himself. This sport don't ask nobody who he is, but while he's buyin' drinks he's telling about others that has gone to these countries and come back with gold in every pocket, an' it ain't long till all have signed up and joined. If there's any danger of them weakening, he keeps them drunk. There's been many a man that got drunk in St. Louis, and when he comes to out of this debauch he's hundreds of miles up the Missouri, on a line dragging a boat loaded with trade goods for the Injun country. If he turns back he's liable to bump into war parties, so he stays. This game is played on sailor, woods and river men. Cowpunchers were of the same kind of goods—all careless, homeless, hard-drinking men.

Fur traders were the first and real adventurers. They went to countries unknown—every track they made was dangerous. On every side were unseen savages. Such people as Colter, Bridger, and men of their stamp, these fellers were not out for gold or great wealth—they asked for little but life and adventure. They had no dreams of palaces. Few of them ever returned. The gold-hunter who came later loved the mountains for the gold he found in them, and some when they got it returned to the city, where they spent it and died in comfort. But most trappers kissed good-bye to civilization and their birthplace—took an Injun woman, and finished, nobody knowed how or where.

The cowboy was the last of this kind, and he's mighty near extinct. He came from everywhere—farms, big cities, and some of them from colleges. Most of them drank when they could get it.

As I said before, they're all Injuns now since the Volstead law. Just the other day I'm talking to a friend. Says he, "It's funny how crazy an Injun is for whiskey. A few days ago I'm riding along—I got a quart of booze in my saddle pocket. I meet an Injun. He sees what I got, and offers me the hoss he's riding for the quart. To a man that wants a saddle hoss, this one is worth a hundred dollars. I paid six for this moonshine."

"Did you make the trade?" says I.

"Hell, no!" says he. "It's all the booze I got!"

S IZIN' Pete Van up from looks," says Rawhide Rawlins, "you'd never pick him for speed, an' I, myself, never see Pete make a quick move without a hoss under him. If Pete's entered in a footrace most folks would play him with a copper, but Bill Skelton claims Pete's the swiftest animal he ever see, barrin' nothin'. At that Bill says he never saw Pete show speed but once, an' that's back in about '78.

"They're in the Musselshell country, an' one mornin' they're out after meat. They ain't traveled far till they sight dust. In them days this means Injuns or buffalo. This makes 'em cautious, 'cause they ain't anxious to bump into no red brothers with a bunch of stolen hosses. When Injuns are traveling with this kind of goods it ain't safe to detain 'em, an' Pete an' Bill both are too genteel to horn in where they ain't welcome, 'specially if it's a big party. Of course, if it's a small bunch they'd be pleased to relieve them by the help of their rifles.

"They start cayotin' around the hills till they sight long strings of brown grass-eaters—buffalo. This herd ain't disturbed none—just travelin'. This means meat an' plenty of it, so gettin' the wind right, they approach.

"The country's rough, an' by holdin' the coulees they're within a hundred yards before they're noticed. It's an old bull that tips their hand; this old boy kinks his tail and jumps stiff-legged. This starts the whole bunch runnin', but it ain't a minute till Pete and Bill's among 'em.

"Pete singles out a cow an' Bill does the same. Pete's so busy emptyin' his Henry into this cow that he forgets all about his saddle.

35

He's ridin' an old-fashioned center-fire. His hoss is young an' shad-bellied, an' with a loose cinch the saddle's workin' back. The first thing Pete knows he's ridin' the cayuse's rump. This hoss ain't broke to ride double an' objects to anybody sittin' on the hind seat, so he sinks his head an' unloads Pete right in front of a cow.

"Bill, who's downed his meat, looks up just in time to see Pete land, and he 'lights runnin'. Bill says the cow only once scratches the grease on Pete's pants. From then on it's Pete's race. It looks like the cow was standin' still.

"Anybody that knows anything about buffaloes knows that cows can run. Pete don't only beat the cow, but runs by his own hoss, which by this time is leavin' the country.

"'Pete's so scared,' says Bill, 'that I damn near run my own hoss down, tryin' to turn him back.'"

"PETE LANDS RUNNING"

"THEY tell me," says Rawhide Rawlins, "that Bill's goin' to build a fine hotel for tourists up on Flathead Lake, not far from where his ranch is. I stayed with him a time or two when he's runnin' that big hotel in Great Falls, an' he sure savvies makin' folks comfortable.

"You wouldn't ever figger that Bill would be runnin' one of these fine modern hotels if you'd knowed him when I first run onto him twenty-five years ago. It's hard to recognize Bill in them good clothes, with a white collar an' a diamond as big as a Mexican bean in his tie, if you wasn't told it was the same man.

"Bill was born near Des Moines, Iowa, and as a boy was knowed as the champion lightweight corn shucker of Hog Bristle County. But when he gets to manhood he takes a dislike to work, an' after hoardin' his wages of three dollars a month for eight years, he just naturally steps underneath a freight train one mornin' with his bankroll an' takes a seat on the rods. He gives one lingerin' look at the old homestead and tells the brakeman he can turn her loose.

"Bill finds a pleasant travelin' companion in a noted tourist, Brakebeam Ben, who kindly divides his conversation an' whatever little things he has on him. Some of these last makes lively company for Bill, who finds travelin' pleasant an' makes lots of stops at points of interest along the line. He gets acquainted with several men who wear stars an' brass buttons. They all take a kindly interest in Bill, an' after insistin' on his spendin' a few days with them, show him the railroad tracks out of town and wish him a pleasant journey.

"A year or so later Bill arrives in McCartyville, a town that in them days was about as quiet an' peaceful as Russia is to-day. McCartyville consists of a graveyard an' one or two ghost cabins now, but then it's a construction camp for the Great Northern, an' there ain't a tougher one on earth, even in them times. The most prosperous business men in McCartyville was the undertakers. They kept two shifts at work all the time, an' every mornin' they'd call at the hotel an' saloons to carry out the victims of the night before. No one asked no questions.

"When Bill steps off the train there he has an Iowa thirst, an' he's just as welcome as his remainin' two dollars an' a half, which is good for just ten drinks. To this prohibition-raised boy this is a real novelty, for where he comes from, no one drinks without hidin' in the cellar. Bill tells me that the lives of a lot of his friends there is just one long game of hide-and-seek. In them days an Iowan could drink more in one swaller than the average westerner can in three hours, so Bill's called on frequent by the barkeep to slow up, as they can only make just so much liquor every twenty-four hours.

"It's here Bill gets his trainin' in hotel-runnin', from washin' dishes to dealin' biscuits through the smoke that hangs heavy around the dinin' room. At the end of three days he's told by the marshal to climb the hill an' back-track as far as he likes. Bill said that they didn't like no peaceful disposed citizens there, but I never heard no one else accuse him of this weakness he claims.

"A few days later he lands in Shelby, where the citizens are surprised and delighted to see him separate himself from the rods. He's covered with dust an' resembles part of the runnin' gear. In this way he was able to hide out from the brakies. When he asks for a room with a bath it's too much for the clerk, who has a nervous temperament an' has spent the previous evenin' drinkin' Shelby lemonade, an' he shoots Bill's hat off. This drink I mention was popular among the Shelbyites of that day. It's a mixture of alkali water, alcohol, tobacco juice an' a dash of strychnine—the last to keep the heart goin'.

"This outburst of the clerk don't scare Bill none, as he's been permanently cured of gunshyness at McCartyville. As the clerk lowers his gun, Bill warps a couplin' pin just under where the gent's hat rests. The hat's ruined, but the clerk comes to three days later to find Bill's got his job. This is where Bill breaks into the hotel business. A week later in a game of stud poker he wins the hotel. I never believe the story whispered around by some of the citizens that it's a cold deck that did it.

"Bill's chef's one of the most rapid cooks known in the West. He hangs up a bet of a hundred dollars that with the use of a can-opener, he can feed more cowpunchers an' sheepherders than any other cook west of the Mississippi. There's never no complaint about the meat, either, for this cook's as good with a gun as he is with a can-opener. In fact, no one ever claims he ain't a good cook after takin' one look at him.

"Shelby's changed a lot since them days. In the old times the residents there include a lot of humorists who have a habit of stop-pin' trains an' entertainin' the passengers. Most of these last is from the East, an' they seemed to be serious-minded, with little fun in their make-up. The Shelby folks get so jokey with one theatri-cal troupe that stops there that many of these actors will turn pale to-day at the mention of the place. At last Jim Hill gets on the fight an' threatens to build around by way of Gold Butte an' cut out Shelby, preferrin' to climb the Sweetgrass Hills to runnin' his trains through this jolly bunch.

"This hotel of Bill's was one of the few places I've seen that's got flies both winter an' summer. During the cold months they come from all over the Northwest to winter with Bill, an' hive in the kitchen an' dinin' room. Bill claims they're intelligent insects, as they'll spend several hours a day in warm weather frolickin' around the hog pens, but when he rings the triangle for meals they start in a cloud for the dinin' room. For a home-like, congenial place for a fly to live, you couldn't beat Bill's hotel.

"Bill's run several hotels since this, an' as he's kept on goin' up in the business, this new one he's goin' to tackle on the lake will probably top 'em all, but it's doubtful if he'll be able to furnish as much excitement for his guests as the old place at Shelby used to provide for the boarders."

BILL WARD'S SHELBY HOTEL

TALK had drifted into the days of the buffalo. "I run onto a head yesterday that the bone hunters must have overlooked," said Long Wilson. "It's kinda hid away under the rimrock on Lone Injun. 'Twas an old bull, with the horns gnawed down to the nubs by trade-rats an' there's a little wool on the forehead, bleached an' faded till it's almost white. 'Tain't long ago the country was covered with these relics, but since the bone hunters cleaned up you seldom see one. Down on the Missouri I've seen bunches of skeletons, runnin' from ten to sixty. You generally find 'em under a knoll or raise in the country, an' by scoutin' around a little you might find in a waller or behind a greasewood a pile of long, bottleneck shells. These are Sharp's ca'tridges, an' in number they'd count a few over the skulls. These skin hunters didn't waste much lead; they had killin' down to a fineness, goin' at it in a business way. They hunted afoot, an' most of 'em used glasses. When Mister Skin Hunter leaves camp he's loaded down with ammunition, an' packin' a gun that looks an' weighs like a crowbar. He prowls along the high country till he sights the herd; then gettin' the wind right he keeps the coulees till he sights the range, an' it don't have to be close, 'cause these old Sharp's pack lead a thousand yards. First he picks out a cow on the edge of the bunch, an' pullin' down on her he breaks her back. Of course she starts draggin' her hindquarters an' makin' all kinds of buffalo noise. Quicker than you'd bat your eye, her neighbors 're 'round her wantin' to know what's the matter.

"Buffalo 're like any other cow-brute; kill one, an'they don't notice it much or 're liable to quit the country; cripple one an' start the blood, an' it's pretty near a cinch they'll hang 'round. The hide hunters know this trick an' most of 'em use it. When the herd gets to millin', he goes to work pourin' lead into 'em as fast as he can work the lever on his breech-block. Whenever one tries to break out of the mill, there's a ball goes bustin' through its lungs, causin' it to belch blood, an' strangle, an' it ain't long till they quit tryin' to get away an' stand an' take their medicine. Then this cold-blooded proposition in the waller settles down to business, droppin' one at a time an' easin' up now an' agin to cool his gun, but never for long till he sees through the smoke the ground covered with still, brown spots. Then layin' down his hot weapon he straightens up an' signals the skinners that's comin' up behind. They've located him by the talk of his Sharp's.

"This is what hunters called 'gettin' a stand'; there's nothin' taken off the animal but the hide an' sometimes the tongue. The rest goes to the wolves. These hide hunters 're the gentlemen that cleaned up the buffalo, an' since the bone gatherers come there ain't nothin' left to show that there ever was any. I've seen a few buffalo myself, but the big herds was gettin' pretty seldom when I hit the country. I guess you've all heard them yarns about how they used to stop the boats on the Missouri, an' how wagon-trains would have to corral for days, lettin' a herd pass. The strongest yarn I ever heard of this kind was told by an old feller up on High River Springs. He's a Hudson Bay man, an's tellin' about comin' south from Edmonton with a Red River cart-train. They're just north of the Big Bow when they run into a herd; as near as he can figure there's a couple of million. It's spring an' the calves 're so plentiful they have to stop every little ways an' pry 'em from between the spokes; they keep blockin' the wheels."

"Buffalo?" says old Dad Lane. "I was here when they're thick as hair on a dog, but it's surprisin' how quick one of these big herds could quit a country. You'd travel for days in sight of 'em, an'

"WITH A GOOD HOSS UNDER HIM, IT WAS EASY FOR AN INJUN TO GET MEAT."

OME

NGE

"THE INJUN PULLS MURPHY TOWARD HIM, AND AT THE SAME TIME HIS LEFT
HAND PULLS THE TRIGGER."

wake up some mornin' an' it'd look like they'd disappeared from the face of the earth; you'd ride for ten days without seein' hide or hair of 'em. Whether they walked or run I never knowed, but from looks you'd swear they'd flew. This sudden disappearin' of buffalo comes pretty near causin' me to cash in once.

"I'VE SEEN BUFFALO MYSELF"

"It's back in '62. There's me, Jack Welch, Murphy, an' a feller called Whisky Brown, builds a tradin' post up near Writin' Stone. We're short of goods an' somebody's got to go to Benton; so me an' Joe Burke, an interpreter, knowin' the country, volunteers to make the trip. This Burke's a full-blooded Piegan, but bein' raised by a white man he's tuk his name. He's knowed amongst his people as 'Bad Meat.' Our outfit's made up of eight pack-ponies an' two Red River carts. We're drivin' these vehicles jerkneck, that is the trail pony's tied to the lead cart so one man can handle both.

I'm teamster; the Injun's got the pack-train. The first couple of days it's smooth sailin'. It's August, the weather's fine, an' we're never out o' sight o' buffalo, so meat's always handy.

"The second mornin' when we're quittin' the blankets I notice the sun down on the skyline, lookin' like a red-hot stove lid, an' my nostrils fill with the smell of burnt grass, tellin' me the range is afire somewhere south of us. 'Tain't an hour till the sky's smoked up so the sun's hid, an' we've lost our timepiece an' compass. But it don't worry me none; I can see the Injun joggin' along ahead; all the smoke in hell couldn't lose him. There's one place where an Injun holds the edge on a white man—day or night you can't lose him.

"I remember askin' Bad Meat how it was that an Injun never loses his way. He tells me when a white man travels he looks one way, always straight ahead. Passin' a butte, he only sees one side of it, never lookin' back; so of course he don't savvy that butte on his return. The Injun looks all ways an' sees all sides of everythin'. There's somethin' in this, but that ain't all there is to it. Of course an Injun ain't got eyes for nothin', but it ain't all seein', 'cause I've been with savages nights so black that bats stayed to home; but it don't bother Mister Injun. He travels without hesitatin', like it's broad day. I don't know how he does it an' I doubt if the Injun can tell himself. These people 're only part human an' this is where the animal crops out.

"Well, we keep workin' along south through the smoke. Once in a while I can see a string o' buffalo, dim through the smoke like shadows. Sometimes they get right up on us before sightin' our outfit. Then swervin' from their course they go lopin' off an' 're soon lost from sight. Towards evenin' Bad Meat downs a young cow an' while we're takin' the back-meat he advises takin' the hams; but I say 'What's the use? It's only that much extra packin', an' we'll get meat to-morrow.'

A FULL-BLOODED PIEGAN

"'All the buffalo we see to-day is travelin',' says he. 'Maybe-so no meat to-morrow.'

"Since he spoke of it I notice that they are all travelin', an' not so slow either, but I've seen buffalo lope an' trot goin' to or leavin' water, an' didn't think nothin' of it. But takin' Bad Meat's hunch, we take the hams.

"'Bout noon the next day we strike the burnt country. As far as you can see she's black, with now an' then a smoulderin' buffalo chip that still holds the fire. It's a sorry sight; a few hours ago this country wore grass that'd whip a hoss on the knees, an' buffalo fed by thousands. Now she's lifeless, smoked an' charred till she looks like hell with the folks moved out. It's the same all day— black, without a livin' critter in sight. The outlook's bad for the cayuses, but towards evenin' we strike a creek that Bad Meat calls 'Wild Dog,' an' a little patch of grass the fire's gone 'round. The Injun's not for stoppin' except to eat a bite an' water the hosses; then push on into the night away from the fire. Injun-like, he's been houndin' the ground all day an' finds some tracks. He tells me he's seen the moccasin marks, as near as he can guess, of about eight men, an' there ain't no pony sign among 'em; they're all afoot. An' when the sun shows red like a bloody warshield, he says, it's 'bad medicine.'

"This savage superstition about the sun sounds foolish to me, an' I tell him it's the smoke causes it. 'Yes,' says he, 'but who built the fire? We're still in the country of the Piegans; do they burn their own grass?'

"Of course these tracks look bad, 'cause when you see Injuns walkin' in a country it's a cinch they ain't friendly. Walkin' makes all people dangerous. War parties generally travel this way an' by the time they, or anybody else, have walked a hundred miles or so they ain't to be trusted amongst hosses. Me an' Bad Meat talks it over an' decides by puttin' out the fire it'll be safe enough.

Our hosses 're all good to stay, an' barrin' two we hobble an' our herd-hoss on a picket rope, they're all loose. It's been a tiresome day, an' I no more'n hit the blankets till I'm asleep.

"Along in the night sometime I'm awakened by a report of guns. It kind o' dazes me at first; then a ball spats agin a wheel spoke just above my head, an' I ain't slow changin' my bed-ground. Mister Injun had an idee where I'm sleepin' an' is feelin' for me with his gun. He's doin' good guessin' in the darkness an' comes within a foot of findin' me. I'm awake plenty now an' hear the hosses runnin'. By the way the noise is leavin' me I know they're pushin' the country behind 'em mighty rapid. I tell you, boys, it's tough layin' there listenin' to all you got leavin' you, but there ain't nothin' to do. In that country we're as good as blind men. It's the darkest night I ever see, an' the burnt ground don't help it none. I'm so damn mad I blaze away in the dark once at the noise an' think I hear a hoss bawl like he's hit, but I guess it's my imagination, for there's nothin' to show for it in the mornin'. I'm cussin' an' goin' on when I hear Bad Meat kind o' chucklin'. He calls to me from his blankets. 'I knowed it,' says he.

"'If you knowed,' says I, 'you're a little late breakin' the news. What's the cause of you holdin' out all this knowledge?' An' I cussed him up a batch. I'm in the wrong all right, but ain't in no humor to own up to it—'specially to an Injun.

"As I said before, we're helpless, but there ain't nothin' to do but wait for day. When it's light I'm surprised at Bad Meat's appearance. Up till now he's wearin' white man's clothes, but this mornin' he's back to the clout, skin leggin's, an' shirt. His fore-top's wrapped in otterskin an' from his hair to just below his eyes he's smeared with ochre. The rest of his face is black, with green stripes. He notices my surprise an' tells me it ain't good medicine for an Indian to die with white men's clothes. I ask him what's his reason for thinkin' about cashin' in. 'That war-party,' says he, 'is

mighty successful in gettin' them hosses, but all Injuns love to get
some little token to take back to their folks, such as hair.' This
kind o' worries me; I ain't anxious to furnish no savages locks to
trim leggin's with, an' I think Bad Meat feels the same way, 'cause
he says it'll be a good idea to travel nights from here on, an' I second
the motion.

"Bad Meat calls the turn when he says these Injuns ain't
satisfied, for while we're eatin' breakfast there's a band of 'em
looms up on a ridge. It's the same party that makes the night visit;
I recognize the hosses. While we're lookin' 'em over, one buck
slides from his pony, an' restin' his gun on his cross-sticks takes a
crack at us. There's a little curl o' dust out on the prairie shows me
that his old smooth-bore won't pack lead near that distance, but
the way he's pintin' his weapon tells me it ain't no friendly salute,
so me an' Bad Meat takes out the prairie. We don't no more'n
reach the brush till they're all down off the ridge, yelpin' like a band
o' coyotes. Bad Meat starts singin' his war-ditty. On hearin' his
gun bark I look off on the prairie; there lays one still Injun. There's
a loose pony lopin' off with nothin' on but a war-bridle. It's a good
shot for an Injun, but Bad Meat's over average.

"This good shootin' don't seem to pacify these savages, an'
the way they start pilin' lead in our direction makes us hug the
brush; we don't leave it till dark. Barrin' a bundle o' robes Bad
Meat grabs when we're quittin' the camp it's a Mexican stand-off,
which means gettin' away alive. Of course we got our guns, but
we're grubless, an' for three days we don't swaller nothin' more
stimulatin' than water. The fourth mornin' we're out o' the burnt
country. It's gettin' pretty light an' we're thinkin' about campin'
when we see four old bulls about a mile off. The country's level as
a table an' the chances of gettin' near enough for a shot looks
slim. The Injun says he knows a way, an' unrollin' the robes he
comes up with a couple o' wolf-skins. He tells me his granddad used

to play wolf an' fool the buffalo. When we get our disguises tied on we find a shallow coulee that'll save a lot of crawlin'. On reachin' the raise we drop to all fours an' start playin' wolf. The Injun's a little ahead an' when he tops the draw I notice him pull a wisp o' grass an' toss it up. There's so little wind it's hard to tell the direction, but the grass falls just back of his shoulder. Bad Meat signs 'good,' an' we start crawlin'. I'm so hungry I feel like a wolf all right, but for looks I'm no good; my suit's too small an' I keep thinkin' that any buffalo that wouldn't tumble to me must be near-sighted or a damn fool. It's different with Bad Meat. A little way off in the grass he's actin' wolf mighty natural. Injun-like, he knows the animal an's got that side-wheelin' gait of the loafer wolf down fine.

"We ain't gone far when the nearest bull raises his head an' lifts nose, but the wind's wrong an' he don't find nothin'; so after lookin' us over, he goes grazin'. I'm within twenty-five yards when I pick out my bull. They're all old boys that's been whipped out of the main herd, but goin' on looks I draw down on the young-est. I'm half hid in the buckbrush an' he's standin' broadside. His heart's what I aim for, but bein' weak an' trembly from hunger I notice the sight wavin' when I pull the trigger, an' when I look under the smoke there stands the bull with his head up, an' tail kinked. There's a red blotch on his side, but it's too high an' fur back. The bull stands a few seconds lookin'. He can't see me 'cause I'm layin' flat as a snake; it's the damn smoke hangin' over me that tips my hand. I'm tryin' hard to re-load when he comes for me, snortin' an' gruntin'. When I raise to run, the wolf-skin slips down an' hobbles me, an' the next thing I know I'm amongst his horns.

"Lucky for me I get between 'em, an' grabbin' a horn in each hand I'm hangin' for all there's in me, while the bull's doin' his best to break my holt. But bein' shot through the lungs he's weak an' slowly bleedin' to death. I'm playin' my strength agin his'n when I hear the bark of Bad Meat's gun. The bull goes over, an' the fight's mine. Maybe you think that old Injun don't look good standin' there with his old muzzle-loader.

"Barrin' bein' covered with blood an' the bark peeled off me in places where Mister Bull drags me, I'm all right. This bull-meat's pretty strong an' tough, but it's fillin' an' takes us to Benton."

"I'M HANGIN' ON FOR ALL THERE IS IN ME"

BAB'S SKEES

OLD BABCOCK," says Rawhide, "could tell yarns that's scary. We're talking about skees when Bab springs this one.

"'Me and Gumboot Williams are camped on Swimmin' Women,' says Bab. 'We was set afoot by the Crows. It's back in '76—we'd saved our hair and we're hidin'. The snow comes early that fall—we're away up on the Swimmin' Women. There's lots of game, but we're huggin' camp close—we're afraid of war parties, but a little later when we know Injuns have quit prowlin', we get bold. We're right comfortable, but we're running low on meat.

"'It's hard travelin', the snow's so deep. I don't know nothin' about makin' snowshoes so I decide it's easier to build skees, and hew a pair out of lodgepole pine. I try 'em out around camp. I can't make much time, but I keep on top of the snow. It's hard climbing till I wrap them with a strip of buffalo robe, makin' a kind of rough lock. So, one morning, I starts climbing the south side of the Snowies. I'm keepin' to the open country, avoidin' timber. 'Tain't long till I jump five blacktail but don't get a shot.

"'About noon I'm pretty high, and stop to get my wind while I'm viewing the country. It's so clear I can see the Musselshell, 'way south. Suddenly I see about two miles below me, a band of about twenty elk—some of them is laying down. I'm packing a forty-four Henry, so after throwing a shell in the barrel, I slip my rough locks and start, an' it ain't a minute till I know I've lost control. I'm riding a cyclone with the bridle off, or somebody's kicked the lid off and I'm coming like a bat out of hell. I can smell the

51

smoke of my skees. They're sure warming up when I hit astride of a dead lodgepole. It looks like this would stop me, but don't ever think it. She busts at the root, bends over, and when I shoot off the end she's trimmed as slick as a fish-pole—there ain't a limb on her. I must have split about fifty of these when these elk hear the noise. They're leaving their beds when I come hurling off the end of a lodgepole and light straddle of the biggest bull there. I stay with him till he wipes me off with his horns. I land this time sittin' on my skees. I've still got my Henry and I'm fightin' mad. While I'm passin' this bunch they look like they're backing up. I throw down a big cow and break her shoulders. I'm still traveling south but ain't got time to skin my killin'. After trimming several hundred more acres of lodgepoles, the country levels and I slow down and finally quit. From my belt down I'm dressed like a savage, but I'm warm both ways from the middle; I'm plumb feverish. I'm still wearing a belt, and lucky I've got my rough locks. It's easy back tracking—of course, there are long distances there ain't no tracks, but while I'm in the air I'm cutting swaths in the timber that looks like a landslide. When I get to the cow, I take the tongue and loins. I don't reach camp till dark.

"'I think,' says Bab, shaking out his pipe, 'that Injun webs is the best if you ain't in a hurry.'"

MANY TRAILS

THIS yarn, a friend of mine tells—I ain't givin' his name 'cause he's married, and married men don't like history too near home, but I will say he's a cowpuncher and his folks on his mother's side wore moccasins. He tells me he's holding beef for the TL out of Big Sandy. Him and another cowpuncher is on night guard. I'll call this puncher "Big Man."

"We're holdin' about fifteen hundred out of Big Sandy," says Big. "We ain't more than two miles from town, expecting to load. Where we've got 'em bedded, you can see the lights of town, and once in a while I can hear singin' and music. It's a fine night. They've been on good grass all day and they're laying good, so good my pardner says to me, 'Big, if you want to go to town for a while, I'll hold 'em all right.' Says I, 'I won't be gone long, then you can take your turn.'

"It ain't long after till my hoss is at the rack, and I've joined the joymakers. They're sure whooping her up, singin', and I get a little of that conversation fluid in me. I'm singin' so good I wonder why some concert hall in Butte don't hire me. The bartender is busy as a beaver—the piano player's singin' 'Always Take Mother's Advice; She Knows What Is Best for Her Boy.' And, of course, we're all doin' that. I've heard that song where a rattlesnake would be ashamed to meet his mother. But whiskey is the juice of beautiful sentiment.

"A little while before I become unconscious, I'm shaking hands with a feller that I knowed for years but never knowed he had a twin brother. The last I remember, I'm crawling my horse at the rack. Then the light goes out. When I wake up I'm cold as a dead snake, and I'm laying on my belly in the middle of the herd. I'm feared to move 'cause many of this bunch are out of the brakes an' are wild as buffalo and they're mighty touchy. If I'd get up, this bunch would beat me to it, and when they've passed over, my friends would scrape me up with a hoe.

"I can't tell what time it is. It's cloudy and I can't find the dipper. There's one old spotted boy that I recognize—he's a Seventy-nine steer. A few of them are standing. One I see is wanderin' around grazin', but they're mighty quiet. I'm gettin' colder every minute. I'm wantin' to smoke, but I dassn't. I put my head on my arm and doze a little. 'Tain't long. The next time I take a look it's breaking day. And where do you think I am?" says Big Man.

"In the middle of the herd," says I.

"In the middle of the herd? In the middle of hell," says he. "I'm laying in the center of the town dump. The steers that I been looking at are nothing but stoves, tables, boxes; all the discard of Sandy is there. The few that's standin' are tables. That spotted Seventy-nine steer that I know so well is a big goods box. Them spots is white paper. The one I see movin' around is my hoss. He's the only live thing in sight. I got a taste in my mouth like I had supper with a coyote. I ain't quite dead, but I wish I was. From where I am I can see Big Sandy, and from the looks it's as near dead as I am."

CURLEY'S FRIEND

THE yarn I'm about to spring was told to me a long time ago. There's a bunch talking about Injuns, when a feller I'm calling Curley cuts in. "I ain't no Injun lover," says he, "but I'm willin' to give any man a square shake.

"Once I'm runnin' a feed and livery stable at Black Butte. About ten mile out I got a hay camp with a crew of men putting up hay; there's no fences in this country, so I got a hoss herder. This herder is a Bannock Injun; he can't talk much white man, but all the hosses seem to savvy Bannock. I'm feedin' him and his squaw and their bead-eyed boy who's old enough to day herd, and his dad takes 'em nights.

"The old man tells me his name in Bannock, which I don't savvy; but his woman tells it in English talk, that ain't quite as lame as her man's, that it means in my tongue 'Sorry Dog.' So as

57

Sorry Dog, he's on the pay roll. Besides me feedin' him and his family, Sorry Dog's getting $25 a month. This Injun's civilized enough so he wears a hat with the top cut out, but he bars pants; he still wears a clout, leggin's, and blanket like the rest of his folks, besides a shirt I give him that spring. It's a boiled one with a stiff busim which is some soiled. This completes his garb.

"Sorry Dog has a lodge set up where him and his folks is living. The white hands that works for me camps separate in square tents. This Injun has got my work teams throwed in with the town herd which gives him about a hundred head he's herding. As I said before, Sorry Dog can't talk much English but he's got some language hosses seem to savvy, and as he knows just a little more than a hoss they get along fine.

"One evening I ride out to my hay camp. It's a little before sundown I notice a strange Injun in front of Sorry Dog's lodge when I step off my hoss. This Injun walks up holding out his hand. We shake. He's the same as all other red brothers to me but I notice he sizes me up plenty. His pock-marked face is smeared with vermillion, he's wearing a green blanket wrapped to his snaky eyes, an' holding an old Spencer in the crook of his left arm, an' I notice he's shy two fingers on that hand. I savvy, maybe he's lost some folks—it might be one of his women, maybe it's a son, 'cause Injuns like to show their sorrow is on the square an' sometimes hacks off their fingers. It's like white folks tying strings on their fingers so they'll remember what they went after. But when you chop one off you shore won't forget—you'll be sorry for a long time. I see lots of Injuns trimmed this way, so he's no different than others of his kind.

"I guess he camps with his friends all night, but when I'm saddling my hoss next morning I notice he's missing in Sorry Dog's camp. He don't even stay to breakfast. It ain't more than breaking day when I'm saddling, and I notice that Sorry Dog's woman is still building bannocks. I ask where this stranger is. She don't look up from her cooking but says 'He go.' 'Gone where?' says I. 'Lost River,' says she. This river is easy a hundred miles from my hay camp. 'What's he doing here?' says I. 'Come see you,' says she. 'What for see me?' says I. 'Say you good man. Say you not let other man kill his woman.'

"It's three years since what this squaw's talking about happens. It's like this: Me and three other fellers are drifting north from Nevada. We've got ten hosses—there's two that's green bronks, and we're having trouble holdin' 'em. They're bunch quitters. We hobble most of the hosses every night but nearly every morning we're out these two, and we comb the country hunting the quitters we've hobbled every known way, but they've got so they can travel better with hobbles than they kin without. But by the time we're in Idaho the bunch're so trail-worn they stay anywhere, and we're turning 'em all loose but these two bronks.

"One night we're camped in a beaver meadow with grass up to their knees. We've camped there a couple of days, givin' this leg-weary bunch a chance to rest, but we've still got those quitters staked by a front foot to the willows.

"As I said, the feed's good, an' by changing 'em once in a while they're doing fine. We ain't seen anybody white or red since we left Salt Lake, but the second night in this good camp about two o'clock we're wakened an' setting up in our blankets. It's a noise that every man that has lived in this country knows—it's the hoofs of running hosses, and a holler that no human can make but Injuns. This yell will scare a bunch of tired work bulls off the bed-ground.

"Well, we're afoot and there's no use getting up, so we just lay there and talk it over. I've just heard the last hoof beats, when out from the dark I hear a hoss whinner close to camp. 'We ain't afoot,' says Kelly who's sleeping with me. 'That's one of them bunch quitters.'

"Sure enough, when light comes, there they are. If you've got a hoss that will pull a pin, if you'll just tie your stake rope to one of his front feet and the other end to a green willow, pretty well up so as to give it spring, it's a safe bet you'll have a hoss in the morning, as he can't break his rope or pull the willow, an' there's too much spring to hurt him. If these Injuns had of known that, they'd have slipped in an' cut the ropes, but they overlooked a bet and I guess they thought they had 'em all.

"Well, it ain't long till me and Jim Baker—that ain't his name but that's what I'm calling him in this yarn—are trailin' these hoss thieves. Jim is sure warlike—he's one man that likes to kill. I've knowed men that would kill if they had cause, but this Jim kills for the love of killing. It all crops out on him on this war trip of ours.

"These hoss thieves ain't hard to follow. We've kept our stock all shod and we know we're on the right track, but we're slow sometimes. We lose the trail and pick it up again. It's dark when we locate their camp. It looks like a small hunting party—they ain't even got a lodge. We can't see nothing but a brush wickey-up and we can't tell how many there are. Baker's for opening the ball right away, but I talk him into waiting till daylight.

"These Injuns don't think they're followed—they think we're plumb afoot, and are careless. This ain't no regular war party, 'cause I see a woman pass between me and the firelight once in a while, and war parties don't often have shes among 'em. I whisper this to Baker an' he says they're all alike to him, an' I knowed by the growl in his voice what he means. He's itchin' to kill. 'When I'm killin' lice, I don't play no favors,' says he.

"We're laying in the brush in sight of the camp. These Injuns are laughin' and talkin', but I ain't able to make out their number. It's about midnight when I doze off. The bark of a gun wakens me, and there stands Baker with his gun still smoking. It's moonlight and I can see this camp plain, an' there's an Injun laying still right in front of the brush wickey-up. I ain't more than looked till Baker's gun speaks and there's another one down. They're all running for a patch of brush, but when Baker kills his second Injun, I see they're only three women left. They see they can't make it to this shelter an' the three turns towards us with their hands up, calling for mercy, but this don't soften Baker none. He downs one while her hands are up, an' before I can stop him he's got another bead on 'em, when I get to him and kick the gun out of his hand just as his cartridge busts. His shot goes wild—he's squatted, using his knee as a rest, making his shots dead sure, when I kick his gun. I'm war-like myself an' I kick fur enough back to get his hand with my heel. The look he gives me don't show no sweetness. He's using a needle gun, an' he reaches for it again, at the same time tellin' me a few things he thinks about me. I stand for all this, but when his hand goes for another cartridge then I block his game and tell him if he makes another break I'll blow a hole in him that these squaws can walk through. He takes one look at me and he knows my Henry has a full magazine. I make him drop his cartridge belt and walk away from it.

"One of these squaws is young, the other old an' wrinkled. I tell the young one in signs to take my hoss and round up all the hosses. Both these women are so scared the white shows under their paint, but they savvy I'm their friend an' it ain't long till she's got all the hosses in. These Injun hosses with those they stole from us makes about twenty head. All ours are there. I give three to the women and tell them to light out. They pack some grub on their extra hoss, the old woman shakes hands with me, and they make their get-away.

"Baker is standing there all the time cussin' me, and the things he's calling me ain't nice to listen to. But I got his cartridge belt, and with his empty gun he's harmless as a pet rabbit. Well, when we get to camp that night Baker ain't quite so frothy. The rest of

"HE SHOOK HANDS AGAIN AND TOLD ME TO GO"

the boys sees all these hosses, and when I tell them why I'm wearing Baker's belt they all take sides with me. They don't mind killing Injuns, but when I tell them about them squaws coming with their hands up, this softens 'em and they're all my way, so Baker don't get his belt back until several days later he rides up to me and shakes hands and says he is wrong. Then I give him ammunition but with the understanding that if he makes one crooked break we'll all turn on him, so he stays square.

"We all winter in Virginia City, but we're split up—me and Murphy's batchin' together. I see Baker once in a while—he's pleasant enough, but I ain't forgot the looks given me when I kicked the gun out of his hand, and I never feel safe with my back to him.

"One night Baker's playin' the bank and quarrels with another feller. This feller was quicker than Baker, which was the end of the killin'est man I ever knowed, and to tell the truth I don't miss Baker none and feel a whole lot easier. I'd near forgot about him when Sorry Dog's woman tells me why this strange Injun comes so far to see me.

"A year after this happens I'm on my way back to Black Butte from this same ranch. I ain't more than started, when I bump into a band of twenty-five of the most disagreeable-looking Injuns I ever see. The minnit they sight me they pull their ponies down to a walk an' start peelin' their guns. They're about a hundred yards off when they all stop, and one of them starts talking in his own tongue, which I don't savvy. Finally he comes to me alone. He's stripped to the waist and painted yeller and green and he looks nastier than a Healy Monster. When he rides up close he tells me in sign he's my friend. There's nothing about him that looks like friendship and I watched for some crooked move, when I get a flash of his left hand. It's shy two fingers. This makes me look closer and I notice pockmarks under his paint, and then he tells me he knows me; that I'm his woman's friend; that all his people like me; that my heart is strong; that there's no man among the Bannocks that would harm me.

"The only weapon I got is an old cap-and-ball Colt's. If I didn't waste no lead this might get six, but there's anyhow twenty-five. So, when this savage tells me all Bannocks are my friends, he shook hands again and again and told me to go, and I took his word for it.

"Next day the whites are all coming into Black Butte, telling about the Bannock outbreak. Them Injuns done a lot of killing before they stopped a little ways from where they met me. They killed four whites.

"I heard that all good Injuns were dead ones. If that's true, I'm damn glad the one I met that day was still a bad one."

AN INDIAN DANCER

SCHOOL days, school days, dear old Golden Rule days—that's the song I've heer'd 'em sing," says Rawhide Rawlins, "an' it may be all right now, but there was nothin' dear about school days when I got my learnin'. As near as I can remember them he-schoolmarms we had was made of the same material as a bronco-buster. Anyway the one I went to in Missouri had every kid whip-broke. He'd call a name an' pick up a hickory, an' the owner of the name would come tremblin' to the desk.

"Charlie Mix—maybe some of you knowed him—that used to run the stage station at Stanford, tells me about his school days, an' it sure sounds natural. As near as I can remember, he's foaled back in the hills in New York state. There's a bunch of long, ganglin' kids in this neck of the woods that's mostly the offspring of old-time lumber jacks that's drifted down in that country, an' nobody has to tell you that this breed will fight a buzz-saw an' give it three turns the start.

"These old grangers bring in all kinds of teachers for this school, but none of 'em can stay the week out. The last one the kids trim is pretty game an' is over average as a rough-an'-tumble fighter, but his age is agin him. He's tall an' heavy in the shoulders like a work bull, an' he wears long moss on his chin which he's sure proud of, but it turns out it don't help him none to win a battle. Two or three of these Reubens would be easy for him, but when they start doublin' up on him about ten strong, one or two hangin' in his whiskers, another couple ham-stringin' him and the rest swingin' on him with slates, it makes him dizzy. Eye-gougin' an' bitin' ain't barred either, an' this wisdom-bringer has got the same chance of winnin' as a grasshopper that hops into an anthill. He comes to the school in a spring buggy with a high-strung span of roadsters, but he leaves in a light spring wagon, layin' on a goosehair bedtick, with several old ladies bathin' his wounds. The team is a quiet pair of plow animals, an' the driver is told to move along slow an' avoid all bumps.

"It looks like a life vacation to the boys, but the old folks think different. They don't 'low to have their lovin' offspring grow up into no ignorant heathen. So one night these old maws an' paws pull a kind of medicine smoke, an' two of the oldest braves is detailed to go to the big camp, work the herd an' cut out a corral boss for these kids. They go down to New York City, an' after perusin' aroun' they locate a prize-fighter that's out of work. They question him, an' findin' he can read an' write an' knows the multiplication table, they hire him.

"Next morning, Mix tells me, teacher shows up an' the boys are all there itchin' to tear into him. But Mix says there's somethin' about this teacher's looks that makes him superstitious. Of course he don't say nothin'—not wantin' to show yaller—but somehow he's got a hunch that somethin's goin' to happen.

"This gent's head is smaller than's usual in humans. There don't seem to be much space above his eyes, an' his smile, which is meant to be pleasant, is scary. There's a low place where his nose ought to be, an' he could look through a keyhole with both eyes at once. His neck's enough larger than his head so that he could back out of his shirt without unbuttoning his collar. From here down he's built all ways for scrappin', an' when he's standin' at rest his front feet hang about even with his knees. All this Mix takes in at a glance.

"When the school room quiets down the new teacher pulls a nice little talk. 'Boys,' says he, 'I ain't huntin' for trouble, but it's been whispered around that this bunch is fighty, an' I'm here to tell you as a gentleman that if there's any battle pulled, you boys is goin' to take second money.'

"The last word ain't left his mouth till one of the big kids blats at him.

"'Come here,' says he, kind of pleasant, to the kid that did it. The kid starts, but the whole bunch is with him.

"The teacher don't move nor turn a hair, but he kind of shuffles his feet like he's rubbin' the rosin. The first kid that reaches him, he side steps an' puts him to sleep with a left hook. The next one he shoots up under a desk with an upper-cut, and the kid lays there snorin'. They begin goin' down so fast Mix can't count 'em, but the last he remembers he sees the big dipper an' the north star, an' a comet cuts a hole through the moon. When he comes to, it looks like the battle of Bull Run, an' teacher is bendin' over, pourin' water on him from a bucket. He can hear what few girl scholars there is outside cryin'.

"When he gets through bringin' his scholars back to life, teacher tells the boys to get their song books an' line up.

"'Now,' says he, 'turn to page 40 an' we will sing that beautiful little song:

"*Every Monday mornin' we are glad to go to school,*
For we love our lovin' teacher an' obey his kindly rule.

"'He makes us sing that every mornin',' says Mix, 'an' we was sure broke gentle.'"

A SHOW INDIAN

THE line camp was jammed to her fifteen by twenty-foot log walls. It was winter, and the storm had driven many homeless punchers to shelter. Both bunks were loaded with loungers, and as cow-people never sit down when there is a chance to lie down, the blankets on the floor in their tarpaulin covers held their share of cigarette-smoking forms. Talk drifted from one subject to another—riding, roping, and general range chat, finally falling to the proper and handy way to carry a rifle.

"I used ter pack my gun in a sling," said old Dad Lane, the wolfer. "They ain't used these days, since men's got ter usin' scab-bards an' hangin' 'em under their legs. Them old-fashioned slings was used by all prairie and mountain men. If you never seed one, they was made of buckskin or sometimes boot leather, cut in what I'd call a long circle with a hole in each end that lipped over the saddle horn. The gun stuck through acrost in front of ye. In them same times men used gun-covers made of skin or blanket. As I said before, I used one of them slings till I near got caught with my hobbles on; since then I like my weapon loose an' handy. I'll tell you how the play comes up.

"It's back in '78, the same year that Joseph's at war agin the whites. Me an' Mormon Murphy's comin' up from Buford, fol-lerin' the Missouri, trappin' the streams an' headin' toward Ben-ton. This Murphy ain't no real Mormon. He's what we'd call a jack-Mormon; that is, he'd wintered down with Brigham an' played Mormon awhile. He's the best natured man I ever knowed, always wearin' a smile an' lookin' at the bright side of things. We'd wood-hawked, hunted an' trapped together for maybe four years, an' I never heered 'im kick on nothin'. He claims when a man's got his health he's got no licence to bellyache. Murphy's good-hearted till he's foolish, an' so honest he thinks everybody else is on the square. He says if you treat folks right, nobody'll bother you. It's a nice system to play, but I arger it won't do to gamble on. There is men that'll tell ye when ye've tipped yer hole-card, but they're long rides apart. This same confidence in humans is what gets Mormon killed off.

"Well, as I said before, we're trappin' along an' takin' it easy. In them days all a man needs is a shootin'-iron an' a sack of salt to live. There's nothin' to worry us. We're in the Gros Ventres' country, but they ain't hoss-tile, an' we're never out o' sight o' meat—the country's lousy with game.

"One mornin' we're joggin' along at a good gait. It's late in the fall, an' ye know cool weather makes hosses travel up good, when ol' Blue, one of the pack-hosses, throws up his head an' straightens his ears like he sees something, an' when a hoss does this, ye can tap yerself, he ain't lyin'. So I go to watchin' the country ahead where he's lookin'.

"Sure enough, pretty soon there's a rider looms up out of a draw 'bout half a mile off. It's an Injun—I can tell by the way he swings his quirt an' is diggin' his heels in his pony's belly at every step. There's a skift of snow on the country an' he shows up plain agin the white. When he gits clost enough he throws up his hand an' signs he's a friend. Then I notice he's left-handed—anyhow, he's packin' his gun that-a-way. It's in a skin cover stuck through his belt, Injun fashion, with the stock to the left, but what looks crooked to me after sizin' him up is that his quirt hangs on his right wrist.

"With hand-talk I ask him what he is; he signs back 'Gros Ventre.' This Injun looks like any other savage; he's wearin' a white blanket capote with blue leggin's of the same goods. From the copper rim-fire cattridges in his belt, I guess his weapon's a Henry. Now what makes me think he's lyin' is his pony. He's ridin' a good-lookin' but leg-weary Appalusy, an', as I know, these hosses ain't bred by no Indians east o' the Rockies. 'Course all Injuns is good hoss-thieves an' there's plenty o' chance he got him that-a-way, but the Umatilla camp's a long way off, an' these peculiar spotted ponies comes from either there or Nez Perce stock.

"Well, he rides up, an' instead o' comin' to my right an' facin' me, he goes roun' one o' the pack-hosses an' comes quarterin' behind me to the left, his hoss pintin' the same as mine, an' holdin' out his hand says, 'How!' with one o' them wooden smiles. Ye know ye can't tell what an Injun's got for a hole-card by readin' his countenance; winner or loser he looks the same. I shuk my head—someway I don't like this maneuver; I don't know what his game is, but ain't takin' no chances.

"He looks at me like his feelin's is hurt, swings around behind my hoss an' goes to Murphy the same way. Then I'm suspicious an' hollers to Murphy:

"'Don't shake hands with that savage,' says I.

"'What are ye afeard of?' says he, holdin' out his hand an' smilin' good-natured. 'He won't hurt nobody.' Them's the last words Mormon ever speaks.

"It's the quickest trick I ever seed turned; when they grip hands, that damn snake pulls Murphy toward him, at the same time kickin' the Mormon's hoss in the belly. Naturally the animal lunges forward, makin' Murphy as helpless as a man with no arms. Like a flash the Injun's left hand goes under his gun-cover to the trigger. There's a crack, an' the smell of burnt leather an' cloth.

"Murphy ain't hit the ground before that Injun quits his hoss, an' when he lands he lands singin'. I savvy what that means—it's his death song, an' I'm workin' like a beaver to loosen my gun from that damn sling. Maybe it ain't a second, but it seems to me like an hour before it's loose an' I'm playin' an accompaniment to his little ditty. This solo don't last long till I got him as quiet as he made the Mormon.

"When the Injun first rides up, he figgers on downin' me fust. He's a mind reader an' the smilin' Mormon looks easy. Seein' his game blocked, he takes a gamblin' chance. He'd a-got me, too, but the lever on his Henry gets foul of the fringe on the cover, an' I got him on a limb.

"Yes, I planted my pard, all right, but as I ain't got nothin' to dig a grave with bigger 'n a skinnin'-knife, I wraps him in his blanket an' packs him down to a washout an' caves a bank on him. When I takes a last look at him, he seems to be smilin' like he forgives everybody. I tell ye, fellers, I don't know when I cried, it's been a long time ago, an' I didn't shed no tears then, but I damn nigh choked to death at that funeral.

"I've helped plant a whole lot of men one time an' another in my career, but this is the only time I did it single-handed an' lonesome. It's just me an' the hosses, but I'll tell ye I'm damn glad to have them. When ye ain't got humans ye'll find animals good company.

"No, there ain't no prayers said; I ain't used none since I was weaned, an' I've forgot the little one my mammy learnt me. But, I figure it out this way, there ain't no use an old coyote like me makin' a squarin' talk for a man as good as Mormon Murphy. So I stand for a minut with my head bowed like whites do at funerals. It's the best I can do for him. Then I go to the hosses a-standin' there with their heads down like they're helpin' out as mourners, especially Murphy's with the empty saddle an' the gun still in the sling, pulled away off to one side where the helpless Mormon makes his last grab.

"I don't scalp the Injun—not that I wouldn't like to, but I

ain't got time to gather no souvenirs an' I'm afeared to hang around, 'cause Injuns ain't lonesome animals; they band up, an' it's safe bettin' when we see one there's more near by. If I'd a-tuk a head and tail robe off'n him, I'd a-peeled him to his dew-claws, but as it is I'm nervous an' hurried, an' all I got 's his hoss an' gun an' four pair of new moccasins I found under his belt.

"Guess this Injun's a Nez Perce, all right, because a short time after the killin' of Murphy there's a bull-train jumped an' burned on the Cow Creek, an' it ain't long till Joseph surrenders to Miles over on the Snake."

"HIS HOSS STOPS ON THE END OF THE ROPE"

LEPLEY'S BEAR

OLD MAN LEPLEY tells me one time about a bear he was near enough to shake hands with but they don't get acquainted. He's been living on hog side till he's near starved. So, one day he saddled up and starts prowling for something fresh. There's lots of black-tail in the country but they have been hunted till they are shy, so after riding a while without seeing nothing he thinks he'll have better luck afoot. So, the first park he hits, he stakes his hoss. It's an old beaver meadow with bluejoint to his cayuse's knees, and about the center (like it's put there for him) is a dead cottonwood snag handy to stake his hoss to.

"After leaving the park he ain't gone a quarter of a mile till he notices the taller branches of a chokecherry bush movin'. There's no wind, and Lepley knows that bush don't move without something pushing it, so naturally he's curious. 'Tain't long till he heap savvys. It's a big silvertip and he's sure busy berrying. There's lots of meat here, and bear grease is better than any boughten lard. So, Lepley pulls down on him, aimin' for his heart. Mr. Bear bites where the ball hits. It makes Old Silver damn disagreeable—he starts bawlin' and comin'.

"As I said before, there ain't no wind. It's the smoke from his gun hovering over Lepley that tips it off where he's hiding. He's packing a Sharp's carbine an' he ain't got time to reload, so he turns this bear hunt into a foot race. It's a good one, but it looks like the man'll take second money. When he reaches the park his hoss has grazed to the near end. Lepley don't stop to bridle, but leaps for the saddle.

"About this time the hoss sees what's hurrying the rider. One look's enough. In two jumps, he's giving the best he's got. Suddenly something happens. Lepley can't tell whether it's an earthquake or a cyclone, but everything went from under him, and he's sailin' off; but he's flying low, and uses his face for a rough lock, and stops agin some bushes. When he wakes up he don't hear harps nor smell smoke. It ain't till then he remembers he don't untie his rope. The snag snapped off, and his hoss is tryin' to drag it out of the country, and Mr. Bear, by the sound of breaking brush, is hunting a new range and it won't be anywhere near where they met. When his hoss stops on the end of the rope, that old snag snaps and all her branches scatter over the park. I guess Mr. Bear thinks the hoss has turned on him. Maybe some of them big limbs bounced on him and he thinks the hoss has friends and they're throwing clubs at him. Anyhow, Mr. Bear gives the fight to Lepley and the hoss.

"Lepley says that for months he has to walk that old hoss a hundred yards before he can spur him into a lope, and that you could stake him on a hairpin and he'd stay."

"AIN'T you ever heard how Louse Creek got its name?" inquires Rawhide Rawlins. "Well, I ain't no historian, but I happen to savvy this incident. The feller that christens it ain't like a lot of old-timers that consider it an honor to have streams an' towns named after 'em. His first name's Pete, and he still lives in the Judith, but I ain't goin' no further exceptin' to say he's a large, dark-complected feller, he's mighty friendlv with Pat O'Hara, and his hangout is the town of Geyser.

"When I knowed him first he's a cowpuncher. From looks you'd say he didn't have nothin' under his hat but hair, but what he knows about cows is a gift. Right now he's got a nice little bunch rangin' in the foothills. There's a lot of talk about the way he gets his start—you can believe it or not, suit yourself—but I think it's his winnin' way among cows. He could come damn near talkin' a cow out of her calf. Some say they've seen calves follerin' his saddle hoss across the prairie. One old cowman says he's seen that, alright, but lookin' through glasses, there's a rope between the calf and Pete's saddle horn.

"But goin' back to the namin' of Louse Creek, it's one spring roundup, back in the early '80s. We're out on circle, an' me an' Pete's ridin' together. Mine's a center-fire saddle, and I drop back to straighten the blanket an' set it. I ain't but a few minutes behind him, but the next I see of Pete is on the bank of this creek, which didn't have no name then. He's off his hoss an' has stripped his shirt off. With one boulder on the ground an' another about the same size in his hand, he's poundin' the seams of the shirt. He's so busy he don't hear me when I ride up, and he's cussin' and swearin' to himself. I hear him mutter, 'I'm damned if this don't get some of the big ones!'

"Well, from this day on, this stream is known as Louse Creek."

"A BOUNTY IS PLACED ON A
NUMBER OF CITIZENS"

OVER in Lewistown there's a gent livin' that's one of the leadin' citizens. I ain't tippin' his hand by mentionin' no names, but if I'd ever told what I know about him he'd be makin' hair bridles to-day," said Rawhide Rawlins. "We'll call him Johnny an' let it go at that.

"A hoss-wrangler by perfession, he has a natural gift for cookin' an' a keen affection for a Dutch oven, but in them crude days his qualities as a chef ain't appreciated by his rough, uncouth comrades in Yogo Gulch, where when I first knowed him he's leadin' a happy, care-free life, watchin' the miners strugglin' to wrest gold from the unyieldin' rocks. I remember one finicky proposition in the camp that objects to Johnny's pet rats livin' in the flour sack.

"Johnny's got such a good opinion of his own cookin' he hangs up a standin' bet that he can outcook any man in Montana, barrin' Dirty Mike, a chef of the Sour Dough School, who's got a sensitive disposition and is impulsive with a gun. One record Johnny points to is a vinegar pie he bakes at Yogo. It seems that while the pie's in the oven, a prospector, Bedrock Jim, with whom he's bachin', puts some giant powder in with the pie to thaw it out. The powder, likely becomin' jealous of the pie, cuts loose and scatters the cabin for miles up and down the gulch. They find one stove lid on Lost Fork, and the pan the pie's in is missin', but there where the cabin once stood is Vinegar, himself, without even a scar.

"Bein' discouraged in his light cookin', an' never workin' as long as he can get anything else to do, Johnny begins figgerin' out a soft way of makin' a livin'. His pious disposition inclines him toward missionary work, finally, and he picks out the Little Rockies as the most promisin' district to begin reformin'. He starts a revival there that's a cross between Mormonism an' a Sioux ghost dance, but this brand's too tough for even the citizens of this section.

"In them days Landusky is the principal town in the Little Rockies, an' it's a sociable camp, life there bein' far from monotonous. The leadin' industries is saloons an' gamblin' houses, with a fair sprinklin' of dance halls. For noise an' smoke there wasn't nothin' ever seen like it before the big fight in Europe starts. Little lead's wasted, as the shootin's remarkably accurate an' almost anybody serves as a target.

"The mayor, Jew Jake, has lost one hind leg in a argument with a sheriff, and he uses a Winchester for a crutch. Funerals in Landusky is held at night under a white flag, so that business ain't interrupted in the daytime.

"It's towards this peaceful village that Johnny rides one day on a hoss that he's borrowed from a rancher who isn't in when he calls. Johnny don't know he's near a town till he hears it a few miles away. Spurrin' his hoss along he suddenly busts into sight of the place, which reminds him of a chromo of Gettysburg he once seen. But Johnny's game, an' mutterin' somethin' that might have been a short prayer, he passes through the firin' line, bein' shy only his hat and a cigarette he was smokin' when he arrives.

"Either the excitement or somethin' he takes for it puts him into a kind of trance for a few days, an' when he comes to he's laid out on a poker table with his head hangin' off. He takes readily to the life of the place, an' picks as his partner Dum Dum Bill, who's got the reputation of bein' a quiet, scholarly man with a lovable character, always shootin' to kill to save unnecessary pain an' sufferin'. Dum Dum's made a hobby of changin' brands on hosses, an' he's done much to discourage gamblin' by makin' it hard, if not impossible, for other players in a game he's sittin' in to win. His end's a sad one. Bein' caught by a war party of Missourians who's had bad luck with their hoss herds, he's strung up to a corral crossbar. As he hasn't got enough weight below his head to break his neck, his end's hastened by tuckin' an anvil into the seat of his pants.

"Johnny, after throwin' in with Dum Dum Bill, does a lot of good as a reformer. It's due to him that the custom of shootin' at unarmed strangers is barred, an' a bounty—a little less than they paid for a wolf—is placed on a number of citizens. As he's in with the reformers, Johnny's name ain't on this list. The bounty claimer has to show both ears of his victims but scalpin' is frowned on as uncivilized.

"Johnny's in much demand for preachin' funeral sermons, but sometimes he ain't got much tact. At one buryin' where the deceased's been killed in a gun battle, Johnny takes as his text, 'When Fools Go Forth to Fight.' The relatives of the corpse get hostile and Johnny has to spend the next three weeks in a stockade he's built around his house for an emergency like this. After a while he's elected mayor, but as he ain't over-good with a forty-five, he don't take the job.

"Some forms of killin' was barred in Landusky, an' when Johnny makes a puddin' for a Thanksgivin' dinner that kills three guests and disables several more, he has to make a quick get-away. He beats a posse to the railroad by a dozen jumps and swings under the rods of a freight train that's passin'.

"I never took no stock in the rumors that was scattered about Johnny afterward joinin' the Curry gang. The Kid once tells me he'd give five hundred dollars for the name of the man that starts this libel against his hold-up outfit."

"STAY IN THAT HOLE, YOU DAMN FOOL!"

SAFETY FIRST! is the big holler to-day," says Rawhide Rawlins, "but how do you know when and where you're safe? These days it's hard to find. A rocking chair looks gentle, but when an earthquake comes along it's no safer nor as safe as a locoed bronk. A bronk might get you in the clear. I never heard of a salmon from fresh water hurting anybody, but out of a can he's often dangerous.

"One time I'm on a coach," says Rawhide. "I'm sitting up with the driver. We're going down a steep grade when the brake pole snaps. The coach starts crowding the wheelers. Playing safe, I jumps. I roll down a bank about forty feet an' stop in a bed of cactus. This driver's a good one and starts playing the silk on his six, and keeps them ahead of the wheels. They don't run twenty-five yards till the man with the ribbons finds an up-grade, straightens his team and stops. The coach is loaded and nobody gets a scratch. But me, that's playing safe —I look like a porcupine, and it takes weeks to pluck me!

"Old Bedrock Jim tells me one time about him and his pardner. They're prospecting in the Big Horns. One morning they're out of meat. They ain't gone far till they jump an elk. It's a bull. Bedrock gets the first shot—that's all he needs. The bull goes to his knees and rolls over. They both walk up, laying their guns agin a log. The bull's laying with his head under him. Bedrock notices the blood on the bull's neck and thinks his neck's broke, but when he grabs a horn and starts to straighten him out to stick him, the bull gets up. And he ain't friendly and goes to war with Bedrock and his pardner. He's between the hunters and their guns. There's nothing to do but give the bull the fight.

"Bedrock makes a scrub pine that's agin a rock ledge. This tree won't hold two, so his pardner finds a hole under the ledge. It's late in the winter; there's plenty of snow and the wind's in the north. There ain't much comfort up this jack pine. When Bedrock looks around, he notices that Jack Williams (that's his pardner's name) keeps coming out of the hole. Then the bull will charge them. Jack goes back but he don't stay long. The bull ain't only creased, and he's mighty nasty. His hair's all turned the wrong way and the way he rattles his horns agin the rocks around that hole tells he ain't jokin'. But Bedrock can't savvy why, when the bull steps back, Jack comes out of the hole.

"Bedrock's getting cold and plumb out of patience, and he finally hollers down from his perch, 'If you'd stay in that hole, you damn fool, that bull would leave and give us a chance to get away!'

"Jack is taking his turn outside. The bull charges. Jack ducks in as the bull scrapes his horns on the rocks. The bull backs away, shakin' his head. This time when Jack shows, he yells up to Bedrock, 'Stay in the hole, hell! There's a bear in the hole.'

"It's near dark when they get away. Bedrock gets on a lower limb and flags the bull with his coat. He's taking a long chance. The footing he's got, if he ever slips, it's good-bye. As I said before, the bull ain't joshing, but he holds the bull till Jack gets his gun, and when he does he sure kills him. He empties his Henry into him and not a ball goes by."

THE worst hoss I ever rode," said Bowlegs, "I rode because I had to. It was a case of ride or lose my locks, an'
I'm still wearin' hair.

"I was born in a cow-country an' raised with a hoss under me.
I've been ridin' 'em ever since, an' come pretty near savvyin'
the animal. Of course I'm a has-been now, but there was a time
when I feared nothin' that wore hair, an' I've rode some bad ones.
This snaky hoss is one I pick up on the range one time I'm makin' a
get-away.

"I ain't goin' into no details, but I'm with a trail outfit when
I get into this jackpot. It's at a dance-house where we've been long
enough for the redeye they're handin' us to get action, an' durin'
an' between quadrilles we're sure givin' full vent to our joy. I'm
gettin' pretty well salivated an' it ain't no wonder, 'cause one drink
of this booze would make a jackrabbit spit in a rattlesnake's eye.

"But we're all peaceful enough till the sport that runs this
hog-ranch objects to the noise I'm makin'. There's a little back talk
an' he tells me if I don't take my gun off he'll make me eat it. He's
a bad 'ombry, already packin' notches on his gun, an' I'm not so
drunk but what I can see the butt of a forty-five peepin' from his
waistband.

"Knowin' this feller's back history, I ain't takin' no chances.
I see his right hand drop; the next thing I know he's on the floor
with a bunch of screamin' women over him, an' I'm backin' for the
door with a smokin' gun.

"It's night, an' goin' from light into darkness that way blinds
me for a second or two, but it ain't long till I got my hoss from a

snortin', whistlin' bunch at the rack. An' the way that old cow-pony pushes the country behind him, it looks like he savvies there's trouble.

"Our wagon's camped about a mile from this burg, an' it ain't long till I hear the bell of the remuda. This saddle bunch is pretty well trail-worn, but I've one tough, long-winded hoss in my string, an' as the one I'm on won't stand a hard ride, I'm thinkin' of changin'. So when I locate the hoss-wrangler, after tellin' him my troubles, he bunches the remuda till I drop the loop on my top hoss. This wrangler's righter than a rabbit, 'cause when he shakes good-bye, he forks over all his cattridges an' what loose money he's got.

"I know the country south of me well enough, but it ain't healthy hangin' too close to the old trail, so ridin' wide of that, I travel the lonesome places. There ain't no wire in the country them days an' it's smooth sailin'. Cattle's plentiful, an' by the use of my six-gun it's no trouble to get beef. Three days later I'm crossin' the Cheyenne country. These people are pretty warlike, they've been havin' considerable trouble with the cowmen an' there's been some killin' done. You bet all you got they'd make it interestin' for any lonesome puncher they bump into. Knowin' this, I'm mighty cautious.

"What's troublin' me most is my hoss. I've covered anyway two hundred miles, an' he's gone tender. His feet's so wore down that once, lookin' back, I notice blood in his track, an' I can't help thinkin' what a snap these savages would have if they'd run onto me ridin' this leg-weary pony.

"About this time I sight a bunch of hosses trailin' in to water. They're all Injun stock, mostly mares, barrin' one big, high-headed roan. If I can only get my string on him I'll be all right, but with this dead-head between my legs, how am I goin' to do it?

"The creek they're headin' for is pretty broken, an' there's a chance to cut-bank him, so droppin' in behind, I trail along easy, like I'm one of 'em. None of 'em notice me much but the roan; he keeps eyein' me over his shoulder, kind of suspicious. He's a rangy hoss with four white feet an' a bald face, one glass eye givin' him a snaky look. His tail's been trimmed out, an' saddle-marks tells me he's been rode.

"The only thing I don't like about him is his brands. He wears an iron everywhere you can burn a hoss—even his neck an' both jaws. He's burnt till he resembles a brand-book. I don't have to tell you fellers that's a bad sign. Whenever you see a hoss worked over this way, it's a cinch he's changed hands a lot of times an' none of his owners loved him. But then, again, if I'm pickin' a hoss for a long ride, give me a bad one. If he's an outlaw, he ain't got me beat none—there's a pair of us.

"When we drop down on the water I'm plenty pleased. It couldn't have been better if I'd had it made to order. She's cut-banked an' rim-rocked up an' down as far as I can see. But the minnit we start down the slope, Mister Roan gets nervous. With his head higher than ever he starts circlin'. He's seen me makin' my loop, an' it looks like he's on to my hole-card. Right here the creek makes a half-circle, with walls on the opposite side from eight to ten feet high.

"These hosses act pretty dry, for the minnit their feet hit the wet, their muzzles go to the water; all but the roan—he's too busy watchin' me. I've got him cut-banked an' he knows it, but's figurin' on breakin' back. The minnit my rope hits the air, he starts for the open, head an' tail up, but the hum of my swingin' rope turns him, an' back he goes through the mares. With one jump, clearin' the creek, he's agin the bank an' tryin' to climb out, but it's too many for him. He's back with a bull rush, knockin' one mare down an' jumpin' over another. He comes out of there like a bat out of hell an's got the whole bunch stirred up now. Reefin' my tired hoss from shoulder to flank, we jump to the gap. I ain't takin' no chances; my rope's tied hard an' fast, an' with one backhand swing my loop settles on his shoulders, but grabbin' the slack quick, I jerk her up his jaws. Then throwin' all my weight in my left stirrup, with my right spur hooked under the cantle to help my hoss, I wait for the jar.

"This old hoss I'm ridin' 's one of the kind that holds with his hindquarters towards the animal. He's spread out an' braced, but bein' weak, when the roan goes to the end of the rope, he's jerked down. The roan's in the air when the rope tightens, an' he goes plumb over, turnin' a summerset an' hittin' the ground with a thud that stuns him, givin' my hoss time to get to his feet.

"'Tain't two seconds till the roan's up and comin' at me through the dust, with his head an' ears up an' tail flagged; he sure looks warlike. Trottin' up within twenty-five feet of me he stops with all feet braced an' whistles long an' loud. He's tryin' to buffalo me. It's the first hoss I ever see that I'm plumb scared of. From looks he's a man-eater; he's got me pretty near bluffed.

"But sizin' up the hoss under me, it's a groundhog case—climb the tree or the dog'll get you. So slidin' from the saddle I start walkin' up on the rope. He stands braced till I reach his nose; then strikes like a flash of lightnin' with both front feet, just touchin' the rim of my hat. By the way his hoofs cut the air, it wouldn't have been healthy for me if I'd a-been under 'em.

"'If that's yer game, I'll head it off,' thinks I, so goin' to my saddle hoss I unloop the McCarthy from my hackamore. An' buildin' another loop, 'tain't long till I got him by the front feet. When I get him hobbled good, I unsaddle my old friend an' start fixin' for high ridin'. From the looks of the roan's hindquarters an' the way he's muscled an' strung up it's a safe bet he'll go in the air some. When I'm bridlin' him he tries to reach me with his front feet, but bein' hobbled, can't do much. He stands humped, but quiet enough when I'm bridlin' him. He can't fool me; by the way his left ear's dropped down an' the look he's givin' me with that glass eye, I savvy he's layin' for me.

"Of a sudden he swings his head a little to the right an' straightens his ears. Lookin' between 'em, I spy a band of about as nasty a-lookin' Cheyennes as I ever see. One look's a plenty; the way they're stripped an' painted, I know they ain't friendly. These Injuns have sighted me now; I can tell that by their yelpin'. They ain't more'n half a mile off, every pony runnin' an' every rider kickin' him in the belly.

"It's sure a case of hurry up, so tightenin' the cinch till the roan grunts, an' loosenin' the footrope, I grab the cheekpiece of the bridle an' pull the roan's head close 'round to me. Grippin' the horn of the saddle an' chuckin' my foot into the stirrup to the heel, I step across him. The minnit he feels my weight, the ball opens.

"Mister Outlaw squats an' then shoots up straight as a rocket —so straight I'm afraid he's comin' back over, but he don't. He lands all spraddled out. The next jump he catches his head, weaves an' sunfishes, hittin' the ground one leg at a time, all stiffened, givin' me four separate jolts. This mighty near loosens me, but hookin' my right spur in his shoulder an' grabbin' leather with all hands, I get back. When he goes up again he shakes himself like a dog leavin' water, an' the saddle pops an' rattles, causin' me to lose my left stirrup. As I never did get the right one, I'm sittin' on his ribs. He'd a-unloaded me all right, but I hear shots from the Cheyennes an' it scares me so you couldn't a-chopped me loose from him with an axe. If he turned summersets in the air he couldn't pile me now. I've made my brags before this that nothin' that wore hair could make me go to leather, but this time I damn near pull the horn out by the roots, an' it's a Visalia steel fork at that. I've heard many a hoss bawl before, but this one roared, an' I believe if he'd a-loosened me he'd a-eat me up. I'm scareder of him than I am of the Injuns, 'cause there ain't a man on earth, white or red, that could hit me with a scattergun while I'm goin' through these motions. The work I'm doin' would make a professional trapeze performer look like a green hand. Sometimes I'm behind the cantle, then I move over in front of the horn. Finally he kicks my hat off— either that or he makes me kick it off.

"I don't know how long this lasts, but I'm gettin' mighty dizzy when the roan raises his head from where he's had it hid, an' straightenin' his back, starts runnin'. Talk about swift hosses— in two jumps I'm goin' the fastest I ever rode; it looks like he's tryin' to run from under me.

"He's sure bustin' a hole in the breeze. Once there's a Chey-enne ball tears the dust off to one side, but it don't scare me none. At the gait we're goin', if a ball did hit me it wouldn't break the hide. It wouldn't no more'n catch up with us. When I look back over my shoulder there's a chain of dust a mile long, an' it appears like the Cheyennes 're backin' up. The wind roarin' in my ears finally brings me to my senses, an' shakin' the hair out of my hands I get the reins an' start lookin' over my layout. The roan's mane's pretty well pulled out from his ears back. My hat an' six-shooter's missin' an' there's one cantle-string tore out, but barrin' these trimmin's we're all right an' there's no kick comin'. The hoss under me can beat these Injun cavayos any distance from a squirrel's jump to the Rocky Mountains, so I bid farewell to the Cheyennes.

"Yes, fellers, that's the worst hoss I ever forked, but that same roan packed me many a hundred miles to safety, an' as I said before, gentle hosses is all right, but give me a snaky one for a hard ride."

ABOUT forty-five years ago a small band of Crows, maybe twenty-five lodges, were camped on the Greybull. As with all plains Indians, horses meant wealth. This camp was rich, for the hills were covered with ponies of all sizes and colors. It was early summer, and among them were many colts.

Two Crow boys squatted on a knoll, wrapped to their beady eyes, one in a white Hudson Bay blanket, the other in a ragged buffalo robe. The hair of both was carefully fashioned in the style of their people—two parts starting over each temple and ending at the scalp lock. The partings were painted bright vermillion, the same as the upper part of the face. The hair between was cropped and stood erect in a brush-like crest. Beneath their robes they wore breech-clouts and leggings, with moccasins. Neither wore a shirt.

These boys were herders, and their ponies grazed at the ends of their elkskin ropes. They not only watched the pony herds, but their keen eyes saw anything that moved for miles around.

The boy in the buffalo robe beat the ground with the elkhorn handle of his quirt and chanted the war song of his father. Suddenly his companion threw his naked arm from under his blanket and signed, "Medicine," at the same time pointing with his chin to a mare that grazed nearby. The animal was a pinto, and the white parts of her coat were painted in a way that means much to red men. Her foretop and tail wore strips of weatherworn otter skin, and braided in her mane was a skin bag that hid the medicine secrets of her owner.

The mare was well known. She was old, but had given many

buffalo horses to her master, and the long-legged colt at her flank
was also a pinto. His short back and deep chest spoke well for his
future years. His were the points of a buffalo horse.

The colt had been acquainted with the world only a few hours,
but he had seen, smelt, and heard many strange things. He had tried
many times to reach the grass with his muzzle, but failed by many
inches. The boys saw this, and Small Shield, the one in the ragged
robe, said his grandfather had told him that it was good when a
little horse did this; he would be strong and would carry his rider a
long way between suns.

It is the life story of this pinto colt that I shall tell you.

His first year was spent close to his mother's flank. One morning not long after the day on which my story begins, there was great
excitement in camp. The pinto colt, which had been given the name
of Paint, saw all the horses among the lodges. The men were
catching their best animals. Some were smearing their mounts with
paint. Most of the hunters rode one horse and led another. The led
horses wore no saddles and sometimes were ridden by naked boys.
These horses were decked with feathers and paint and wore a medicine charm in mane or tail. This might be the full skin of a magpie
or a wolf leg, or possibly a bat's wing, but whatever it was, it meant
luck to the owner of the horse.

The women were also busy, saddling the quieter ponies or har-
nessing them to the long-poled travois. As they left the camp the
hunters were in advance of the women, and as the latter traveled
slower, they were soon left behind.

Paint noticed that after they had gone some distance, a very
old man made a signal and the women ceased talking. Even the
children were quiet. Now all conversation was carried on by the
hands in sign language. Not long after, they topped a ridge, and it
was here that Paint first smelled the dust and heard the roar of a
running herd. The Crows were among the buffalo.

Here the women stopped their ponies. Many of them sang.
It meant meat and robes, which spelled life to these wild people.

Paint stood with pricked ears, watching the scene in the valley
below. It was an old story to his mother, who quietly cropped the
grass. Before long a rider appeared, leading a sweat-covered, pant-
ing pony. Then others came and the women moved down the slope.

Paint saw many brown spots upon the prairie. As they neared
them he saw that these were horned animals, lying motionless,
and he smelled blood.

For five years he lived with the Crows, and himself became a
buffalo horse, wandering from one country to another, always in
the wake of the herds. One night the Crows were camped on
Painted Robe Creek. They were in a dangerous country, a land
where their enemies, the Blackfeet, often came, so the lodges were
placed in a great circle, forming a corral. At night the horses were

AN INDIAN SIGNAL

brought into the enclosure, most of them staked, or picketed, with short ropes.

The Crows had danced, and all slept soundly. A coyote back of a butte barked. It would have fooled any human, but the wind came and told the nose of Paint the truth—it was a man. The dogs knew, too, and many of them howled in answer.

Not long after this, though the night was dark, Paint saw several robed figures among the ponies. They were busy cutting ropes, and a pony, as soon as loosened, would walk quietly from among the lodges. One came to Paint, and after cutting the rope at the picket pin, coiled it and rubbed his neck. Paint knew it was a stranger and snorted; then jumping to one side, he backed into a tripod of travois, which was hung with drying meat. All of this upset and fell against a lodge, awakening the sleepers. But the stranger held to Paint's rope, and crowding him among the other horses, sprang to his back.

The stranger drove his heels into Paint's flanks and flapped his robe, which he had loosened from his body, over the backs of the animals nearest. The horses were all running now. There was much noise. Guns talked with their yellow tongues into the darkness. Women screamed, dogs howled, and men sang their death songs.

A few jumps and Paint, with his rider, was at the edge of the lodges that formed the corral. Gunfire streaked the darkness from most of the lodges, but as no Indian likes to kill a horse both the Crows and their enemies fired low enough to kill a rider, but too high to hit a horse. As Paint passed between the lodges he saw a streak of fire rip the blackness at his side, and he felt his rider clutch his mane and ride as he had seen the Crows at the trading post when they drank something the white men traded them. Then Paint felt something warm and wet on his neck and withers; the rider's legs loosened and his body lurched heavily over the pony's shoulders to the ground, and Paint ran on riderless.

He was glad to leave the lodges. The noise frightened him. He had seen guns and arrows kill buffalo, and this night he felt as though they might kill a horse. They had traveled far and fast when it grew light. The pony saw painted strangers behind him. This was a Piegan war party down from the north, which had surprised the sleeping Crows. When they left Belly River they numbered ten, but now they were only nine. They were mostly young men, led by Bad Wound.

Bad Wound had seen over fifty winters. Time had been good to him, but war had left him not good to look at. He had lost one eye, and a trade ball from a flintlock in the hands of a Crow had broken both jaws, leaving him with a horrible war dimple in each cheek and a crooked mouth.

When the sun came the party halted to change mounts, as the horses under them were winded. The ponies were bunched and each rider dropped his loop on the neck of a fresh one. It was Bad Wound's loop that caught Paint. The war chief looked him over at rope's end, and then signed "good and strong" to his painted companions. Walking up for close inspection, Bad Wound's hand felt the hard, dark brown substance on Paint's mane and withers and knew why his men only counted nine. Then the chief drew the loop from Paint's neck, and slipping his Henry rifle from its skin cover, fired at the pinto as it trotted into the herd. The animal went to its knees; then rolled over and stiffened. "It was not good," said Bad Wound, "to let a friend walk to the sand hills. The trail is long and I have given him a strong horse."

After the warriors had all caught fresh horses they took the herd to a deep, grassy valley, where their mounts were hobbled and all the ponies were watered and allowed to graze. The men then ate their jerked meat, and all excepting two sentinels, who watched the back country, rolled in their blankets or robes and slept.

The sun was low when they moved again, and when Bad

"THE CHIEF FIRED AT THE PINTO"

Wound's one eye passed over the traveling herd, his hand went to his mouth in surprise. He said, "Ghost horse," to a near companion, and pointed to a blood-stained horse in the herd. It was Paint, and his head and neck showed fresh blood. Bad Wound thought his bullet had made a wound that killed, but the lead which was meant for Paint's head had only passed through the neck cord, stunning him for a short time.

They traveled mostly by night, and it was many days before they reached the Piegan camp on the Teton. This was a large camp, a mixture of Piegans, Bloods, and Blackfeet. As far as Paint could see the smoked skin lodges dotted the valley. A scout, or "wolf" as he is called, reported the coming of Bad Wound's party long before his arrival, so when he and his men with the stolen ponies entered the camp, an old medicine man on a much painted pony rode in advance and told the people: "Two moons have come since these men danced with the sun and left their lodges afoot. Their bellies have often been empty and their tracks sometimes red, but they are brothers of the wolf, with strong hearts. When a Blackfoot goes to war he may never return, or his hair may be whitened by winters when he comes, but if he reaches his lodge, whether it has been a few suns or many winters, his feet are not sore, for he has an enemy's horse under him. I have said these are wolves, and the wolf women will give them meat. It is good."

As the party rode into camp hundreds of dogs slunk silently among the lodges. They did not bark, as their only language is the howl of their wilder cousin, the wolf. Every travois and extra lodge pole was hung with buffalo flesh, and the wind was heavy with the smell of meat.

In the Piegan camp there was much feasting and dancing, but there were five with their faces painted black, the father, mother, two sisters, and the young wife of Calf Robe, the one left dead among the Crow lodges. These people did not join in the merriment, out squatted out on the butte, crying and cutting their arms and legs while those in camp sang and stepped time to the big drum. And when the mourners returned to camp, Calf Robe's wife had but two fingers on her left hand. She had given the others to the sun to show her great sorrow.

Then Bad Wound came to Calf Robe's father and gave him three horses and said: "Old Man, I would give you the horse your son rode, but he is a ghost horse. I tried to give him to your son, but the horse would not die. It is not good to give a friend a pony that dead men ride. Three times while I slept the spotted horse came to me. Your son rode him, but he was dead and the pony's back was red with blood. He is a good horse, but I will never ride him. My heart is afraid, and I have said that it is not good to give a friend what you fear yourself."

Next spring the Piegans were camped on a river called The-Banks-That-Fell-on-Them, when a few whites came to buy ponies. Among them was a very young boy and a man with a gray beard, who was the boy's companion. When Bad Wound led out Paint, the boy was much pleased, and Gray Beard counted out forty-five silver dollars into the hand of Bad Wound.

So now Paint had a white master. He had never felt a bit in his mouth before. His bridle had always been two half-hitches of rawhide thong about his under jaw. Also the white man's saddle with its two cinches was strange to him. His back knew only the halfbreed pad and other Indian saddles.

Paint was gentle, but as all Indians mount from the offside, it was days before he would allow the boy to mount from the near side. The pinto pony was not to be alone, as the boy already owned a black mare which packed his blankets and grub.

Some days later, Paint, the mare and their master joined a hunter and trapper who lived in the mountains. One night as they were cooking supper, the old hunter told the boys to trade off the mare. "Lady hosses," said he, "are like their human sisters. They get notions of goin' home, an' no gentleman cayuse would think of letting a lady go alone. Judging from actions, there ain't a cayuse in our bunch that ain't a perfect gentleman, so to play safe, boy, you stake that mare."

A few days later the boy traded the mare for a one-eyed buckskin cayuse.

For two years the boy lived with the hunter. The next time he appears in our story he is wrangling horses for a trail herd which was traveling north. This herd was turned loose on Ross's Fork, where there was a big roundup camp. Here the boy was hired to night-herd four hundred saddle horses. This camp reminded Paint somewhat of the homes of his early wild owners, but the lodges were not tall like those of the Crows or Piegans.

For many years Paint, with his master, followed the white man's buffalo. Once they went north and again the pony was among the lodges of the Piegans. When the big cow herds moved north of the Missouri, Paint and his master were with them.

One night in a little cow town on Milk River, Paint, among other ponies, was tied to a rack in front of a place where cowmen drank, sang, and made merry. The night was warm, and the door was open, so Paint could see inside. There was some hard talk, and Paint knew men well enough to understand that it was war talk of the white man. He saw a man pull a gun and fire twice, then back through the door with the smoking weapon in his hand. Another man lay on the floor very still. The man who had fired the gun stepped to the hitching rack, mounted a horse and rode away into the darkness. Paint knew then that the white man was no different from the red. They both kill their own kind.

Some years later two riders, one leading a pack horse, traveled between the Missouri River and the Highwood Mountains. One of them pointed to a heavy smoke that showed on the horizon, a little south of west. "There's where we camp to-night," said he.

It was dark when they reached the town which the smoke had led them to, and their ponies, which knew no lights but Nature's, jumped the great shadows made by the arc lights at the street crossings. They passed rows of saloons, dance halls, and gambling houses, and after enquiring the way of a bystander, rode to the Park stables, where they unsaddled and stripped the pack horse of their bedding and grub.

Now, under the overhanging light of the stable, I will describe the riders and their mounts. One rider was rather slender with black hair and eyes. The other was of medium height, with light hair worn rather long. Both men were dressed as cow hands, and the only difference in their clothes was a bright colored, French half-breed sash, worn by the light-haired man. The latter's mount was a rangy gray, branded Diamond G—one of the old Geddis herd. The pack horse which he led was a bay pinto.

The darker man rode a brown, strongly-built bronco, which snorted at every strange thing he saw.

The name of this town was Great Falls. The rider of the brown bronc was Henry Stough. The other, who rode the gray, was the writer of this story. The pinto pack horse was Paint, called Monty by his owner.

When Paint died near Great Falls he had been with his master twenty-five years.

MAVERICKS AND STRAYS

RANGE HOSSES," says Rawhide Rawlins, "don't ask nothin' of men. Since Cortez brought them, they've been takin' care of themselves. They've been a long time learnin' —from the land of drought to the country of deep snows and long winters, they ranged.

"The Injuns used to tame wolves to move their camps till the Spaniard came. These dogs bein' meat eaters, it kept the red man busy feedin' his folks and his dogs. It's a cinch that lots of the time the whole outfit went hungry. I'm guessin' that in those days that nobody knows about, the red men followed the wolf and when able, drove him from his kill, and the wolf had the best end of it. But with a noss under him it was different. The wolf followed the red man and got part of his kill. Some Injuns call the hoss 'the big dog,' but I'm tellin' about hosses.

"All other animals cached their young when they went to water. When a colt was born, his mother never left him and in a short time, he would travel with his maw. Wolves don't have much chance. Hosses stay in bands—if a wolf or wolves show up, they won't run like other animals, they bunch; and range hosses are dangerous at both ends, strikin' and kickin'. A wolf likes somethin' easy. After he feels the hoofs of a range mare a few times, he quits—it takes his appetite.

"When winter comes, the range hoss don't hug the brush like cows and starve to death—he hunts the ridges where the snow blows off. When he gets cold, the whole band will run and warm up — if the snow's deep, he paws to the grass. This keeps him warm. Nature gives him a winter coat. Sometimes, when his belly's full, he'll hunt a wind-break. Sometimes a lion will get a colt, but not often. Range hosses like open country, and won't stay in the brush only long enough to water.

"Hosses love pure cold water. In running water, which they like best, most of them drink with their heads up stream, every hoss tryin' to get up stream above the rile. I've seen bands of hosses at a prairie spring waitin' their turn to drink where it was cold and clear. As I said before, hosses like good water, but in countries where water ain't good, they drink anythin' that's wet. In fly time they bunch and stand heads and tails, each hoss using the tail of his pardner as a fly brush. If there's a breeze they hunt high ground; if it's still, they pick bare ground where there's lots of dust. In saddle bands, like you'll see on roundups, hosses will stay in groups from two to four or five.

"Some hosses will stay friends for years; others, like men, are changeable. A band of hosses turn their hind quarters to a rain or snow storm. They will, if driven, face a storm, but it's hard to make them go sideways. Range hosses in a hilly country stand with their heads down hill. You could drive a band of hosses up the steepest kind of a hill but nobody that I ever knowed could drive a bunch

"IN FLY TIME THEY STAND HEADS AND TAILS, EACH HOSS USIN'
THE TAIL OF HIS PARDNER AS A FLY BRUSH"

straight down (that goes with cows, too)—they'd sidle it every time.

"Hosses raised on the plains don't like the mountains, and if there's any chance they pull out. A hoss loves the range where he was foaled and will drift hundreds of miles to get back. If you're traveling with strange hosses, and camp, as long as they are tired and hungry they stay, but if there's a bunch quitter watch him when he fills up—he'll drift and travel.

"Most hosses are good swimmers, but few of them like it. If you want to play safe, swimming a hoss, loosen your cinches and jerk your bridle off. Maybe you won't come out just where you wanted, but you'll come out. Many a man has drowned himself and hoss by pullin' his hoss over. If you're lost in a blizzard, give your cayuse his head—he'll take you to shelter—it's hard to lose an animal.

"In the dark, don't spur a hoss where he don't want to go. There's lots of times a hoss knows more than a man. A man that says a hoss don't know nothin' don't know much about hosses."

"PAW'S GOT HOOF MARKS ALL OVER HIM AN' HE AIN'T
HAD A RIDE YET"

THE HORSE

I READ in the papers a while back where there's seventy thousand wild hosses on the ranges of Montana," says Rawhide Rawlins. "They say these animals are a menace to stockmen. Mebbe this is right, but I think it would bother this old state to round up that many tame ones.

"A few years ago a hoss was considered kind of handy to have around. He was needed everywhere and used all ways. Up hill or down, mud or dust, he worked. They made no good roads for him. There's not a city in mighty near the whole world he didn't help build. There's a few ice-bound countries where the hoss don't live, and in these same lands it ain't easy for humans to live.

"This last war was a machine-made hell, but I doubt if it could have been win without hosses, an' the same kind that some folks say is a menace to men now. There was thousands of branded hosses died with our fighters on the other side. The range hoss was God-made, an' like all of His makin', the best. These hosses cost the man that branded an' claimed 'em nothing. They lived on the grass an' water the Almighty gave 'em.

"Many thousand years ago, when folks was all a-foot, lizards, horned toads, an' bullfrogs measured from thirty to a hundred feet in length an' stood from forty to sixty hands. Besides these, there was tigers and laffin' hyenas that would eat an elephant for breakfast. From what I've read, in the days I'm talkin' about man wasn't much, an' he sure lived simple. A good, stout cave was his home. He fed mostly on bugs an' snails, an' a grasshopper that happened to 'light anywhere near him or his family was out of luck. Sometimes some real game gent would slip out with his stone tomahawk an' bring back a skunk or two. Then's when they pulled a regular feed, but there wasn't no set date for these feasts, an' they mostly came far apart. With a hyena that weighed seven ton a-laffin' around the door, man loved his home, an' Maw never worried about where Paw was.

"But one day one of these old home-livers was sunnin' himself an' layin' for a grasshopper, when he looks down from his ledge to the valley below where all these animals is busy eatin' one another, an' notices one species that don't take no part in this feast, but can out-run an' out-dodge all others. This cave man is progressive, an' has learned to think. He sees this animal is small compared to the rest, an' ain't got no horns, tusks or claws, eatin' nothin' but grass. There's other grass-eaters, but they all wear horns that don't look good to Mister Cave Man.

"He remembers when his Maw used to pack him on her back. Bein' a lazy gent he's lookin' for somethin' easy, an' he figgers that if he could get this hornless animal under him, he could ride once more like he did in his childhood. Right then is when man starts thinkin' of somethin' besides eatin'.

"Not far from the cave there's a trail where herds of hosses come to water, so one day Mister Man climbs into a tree that hangs over the trail, an' with a grapevine loop he snares one of these animals. But he finds out that though this beast ain't got horns or claws, he's mighty handy with all four feet, and when Paw sneaks home that evenin' he's got hoof marks all over him an' he ain't had a ride yet. Sore as he is, he goes back next day an' tries again. About the sixth day this poor hoss is so starved that Mister Man gets up to him, an' tyin' a strip of bark to his under jaw an' another around his belly, he steps across the hoss. The bronc sinks his head an' goes in the air. Mister Man stays, but he breaks all the rules in a ridin' contest of to-day. He don't pull leather, but tears all the mane out from ears to withers, an' that bark hand-hold of his is all that keeps the hoss from unloadin' him. A few days later his bronc is plumb gentle. Paw mounts, goes out an' with a stone-headed spear kills a wild cow, an' he comes back to the cave with the hide an' more meat than the folks ever seen before. The family is so pleased with this useful pet that they bring him in the cave nights, an' all get busy pullin' grass for him.

"Mister Man finds that with four legs under him instead of two, he can ride rings around them big lizards, an' there ain't any of them claw-wearin', tusk-bearin' critters can overtake him. The old gent snares more hosses, an' it ain't long till the whole family's hoss-back. When this bunch starts out, armed an' mounted, they sure bring home the bacon. Meat—I'd tell a man. This cave looks an' smells like a packin' plant before the pure food law. It's now

"THE WHOLE FAMILY STARTS OUT MOUNTED"

mankind sheds the leaf garments of old Granddad Adam an' starts wearin' new clothes.

"Paw's wearin' a head-an'-tail cowskin; the boys has a yearlin' robe apiece. Maw an' the girls wouldn't be in style at all these days. Mebbe it's modesty—it might be the chill in the weather—but they're sure covered from ears to heels in deer an' elk skins, an' from that day to just lately man never knowed whether his sweetheart was knock-kneed or bow-legged.

"Since that old bug-eater snared that first cayuse, his descendants have been climbin', an' the hoss has been with 'em. It was this animal that took 'em from a cave. For thousands of years the hoss an' his long-eared cousins furnished all transportation on land for man an' broke all the ground for their farmin'. He has helped build every railroad in the world. Even now he builds the roads for the automobile that has made him nearly useless, an' I'm here to tell these machine-lovers that it will take a million years for the gas wagon to catch up with the hoss in what he's done for man. To-day some of these auto drivers want to kill him off to make fertilizer out of his body. Mebbe I'm sentimental, but I think it's a damned hard finish for one that has been as good a friend to man as the hoss "

IN THE old days the sight of a cow follered by more than one calf is apt to cause comment among cowpeople," says Rawhide Rawlins. "But times have changed, an' it looks like new improvements has come in the stock business along with dry farmin' an' prohibition. Not all these modern ideas is hatched up on this side of the water, though. Tommy Simpson's prize cow proves that.

"The other day I'm ridin' on Box Elder Creek, when I'm surprised to see a cow that's got five calves follerin' her, all wearin' Tommy Simpson's brand. Tommy's an old-timer in the cattle business, so I figger he'll have some interestin' explanation to make of this miracle. I'm still ponderin' over it when I ride into the town of Fife, which Tommy has named after the village in Scotland that he's run out of as a youth for poachin'. Enterin' the store there, who do I see but the owner of the cow an' five calves. I presently remark that's sure some cow of his.

"Tommy, with both jowls loaded with Climax, as usual, is speechless, until he opens the stove door an' nearly puts the fire out. Then, gettin' his breath, he explains that the cow has been sent to him from the Highlands of Scotland by his grandfather. The animal, he says, comes to this country in charge of a cousin of Tommy.

"It appears that Tommy's cousin, with thrift that's characteristic of the family, drives a sharp bargain with the captain of the sailin' ship in which he engages passage from Strachlachan, which is not far from Ballochantry, somewhere north of the Firth of Galway. Tommy's cousin agrees to furnish milk and cream to the ship's crew an' twenty-three passengers, if they'll let him an' the cow travel on a pass. This suits the captain. On the way over, the cow is milked evenin' an' mornin' by Tommy's cousin an' the members of the larboard watch. How Tommy's cousin an' the cow beat their way from New York to Montana, I never hear.

"Accordin' to Tommy, cows of this breed ain't uncommon in the Scotch Highlands. They're built somewhat along the lines of the lady pig. Tommy says it's an interestin' sight, after the cow gets to his ranch, for the neighbors to watch Tommy and several hired men milk the Scotch cow. The milk from the off side supplies the Fife creamery with butter fat, while that from the near side of the cow nourishes her half-dozen calves.

"Tommy tells me that in Scotland, where these cows eat the nutritious heather, the center bag gives pure cream, the rear one buttermilk, an' the forward one skim milk, so they don't need no separator."

TOMMY SIMPSON'S COW

HANDS UP!

JACK SHEA tells one time about being held up. It was in Colorado, and he's travelin' on a coach. There's five passengers, and one of them is a middle-aged woman. There's been a lot of stick-up men on this road, and this old lady is worried. She's got fifty dollars, and she's tryin' to get to her daughter somewhere up North. This fifty is all she's got, and if she loses it she's on the rocks.

"There's an old man in the bunch that's got all the earmarks of a cowman," says Shea. "He tells her to stick her roll under the cushions, and slips her a couple of dollars, sayin' that it will pacify these road robbers.

"We ain't gone five mile when the coach stops sudden and a gent outside says, 'Step out, folks, an' keep your hands up while you're doin' it.' We all know what we're up against and ain't slow gettin' out. There's one gent at the leaders, got the driver and the outside passenger covered; another that's waitin' for us. They're both wearin' blinds and heeled till they look nasty. This stick-up seems to know the old cowman and speaks to him. The old man steps out of line and whispers something to him. None of us get any of his talk, but when the hold-up gets through trimmin' us he reaches into the coach, flips the cushion, and grabs the old lady's roll. Then we all return to our seats and the hold-up gives the driver his orders and the coach pulls out.

"We're all trimmed; the old lady's cryin', and the rest of us ain't sayin' much, but we're doin' lots of thinkin'. From what we get, it looks like the old cowman stands in with the hold-ups. He's tellin' the lady not to take it so hard. When one of the passengers wants to know what the low talk is between him and the stick-up, the cow-

113

man don't turn a hair but tells us all he double-crossed the lady; that he tells this hold-up that twenty dollars is his bank roll, but if he'll pass him up he knows where there's fifty. The hold-up agrees, and he tips off the old lady's cash to protect himself. He tells it like he ain't ashamed, and finishes, sayin', 'If you don't take care of yourself, nobody else will.'

"This talk makes the whole bunch wolfy. The passenger that's doin' the talkin' is for stoppin' the coach, and if there's a rope there'll be a hangin'. 'We don't need no rope; what's the matter with a lead rein? If he's as light in pounds as he is in principle, we'll slip a boulder in his pants to give him weight. This skunk is dirtier

A STICK-UP ON THE ROAD

than airy hold-up on the road, and the sooner we pull this party, the better it suits me.'

"We're gettin' worked up on all this talk when the cowman that ain't turned a hair, says, 'If you gentlemen will let me play my hand out you'd find out who wins, but if you're bound to, go through with this hangin'.'

"By this time, the old lady's beggin' for the cowman. She don't want to see him strung up, but thinks jail is strong enough. But these passengers are frothin' at the mouth, and it sure looks like the cowman's end is near. The driver has heard the story and stopped.

"'Well,' says the old man, 'if you're bound to hang me—' and he don't scare worth a dam'—'I'll slip my boots. I've been a gambler all my life,' says he, draggin' off his right boot, 'but none of you shorthorns ever was; you never played nothin' but solitaire. This lady stakes me to fifty,' says he, 'and I always split my winnin's in the middle with them that stakes me.' And takin' a thousand dollars he's got tucked in his sock, he counts off five one-hundred-dollar bills, and hands them to the lady. 'That's yours,' says he.

"Nobody says nothin'. The old lady's shakin' hands, and, between sobs, thankin' this old cross-roader. Somebody tells the driver to drive on, and we're just pullin' into town when the man that's strong for hangin' pulls a pint from his hip and says, 'To show you there's no hard feelin's, we'll all take a drink—barrin' the lady.' When the bottle comes back to its owner, it's near dry, but before he empties it, he says, 'Here's to the gambler that pays his stakes!' Then he empties her and throws her out the window, and we all shake hands."

"HE'S WEARIN' THE GARMENTS
OF A BREED"

MORMON ZACK, FIGHTER

I SEE Mormon Zack's in the hospital with a bad front foot. This bein' crippled ain't nothin' strange for the Mormon," said Rawhide Rawlins, as he pulled the makin's out of his coat pocket and started rollin' one.

"If I knowed the story of every scar he's got, I could hand the people a history that would make a lot of the scraps the Kaiser lost look like a prayer meetin'. My knowledge of history's a little hazy, but knowin' Zack came from Norway and judgin' from his actions, he's a come-back of some of them old fightin' Norsemen. You might lick him, but you can't keep him licked, and he fights as well underneath as he does on top.

"The first time I see Zack I'm a kid, helpin' throw up a log shack on the Judith River. There's a feller rides up with an Injun hoss under him. He's sittin' in an old-fashioned low-horn saddle with 'doghouse' stirrups. In dress he's wearin' the garments of a breed—moccasins and beaded buckskin leggin's that come to the knees. In his ca'tridge belt is a skinnin' knife, an' across the front of him lays a Winchester in a fringed an' beaded skin gun-cover. One of the men that's with me tells me that's Mormon Zack.

"That'll soon be 40 years ago. At that time there's still a lot of Injun trade in the country, an' that's the Mormon's business. The first time I knowed of Zack gettin' warlike is a little while after this at Reed's fort, a tradin' post near where Lewistown stands to-day. It's run by Reed and Bowles.

"There's about 200 lodges of Piegans come to the post for trade. Bowles don't happen to be there, as he's gone to Benton to get whiskey. While he's off gettin' this wet goods, Zack an' his partner comes along and make a trade, an' when Bowles arrives there ain't as much as a skunk skin left among them Piegans. They're traded down to a breech-clout.

"This don't make Bowles pleasant to get along with, an' he starts fillin' up on this trade whiskey. This is the booze that made the jack-rabbit spit in a wolf's eye.

"As I said before, Bowles fills up an' starts tellin' Zack how much he thinks of him, an' the talk Zack comes back with ain't very genteel. Zack's standin' pretty close, for all the time they're talkin' he's onto Bowles' hole-card. He knows this hog-leg that's hangin' on Bowles' hip ain't no watch-charm, so to avoid any mis-understanding Zack hands Bowles one on the chin, knockin' him from under his hat. He's near bein' too late, for Bowles has already reached for his barker an' just when Zack's reachin' his jaw she speaks out loud, the ball nearly tearin' Zack's hind leg off at the hip.

"Bowles don't come to till next day, an' then he wants to know which hoss kicked him. Zack's worse off, as there ain't no doctor nearer than Benton. Of course, there's a medicine man in the

"THERE'S STILL A LOT OF INJUN TRADE IN THE COUNTRY"

Piegan camp, but Zack ain't Injun enough to believe that this red doctor can beat a tom-tom an' sing his leg together, so he forks a hoss an' pulls for the steamboat town. This little incident don't seem to take none of the fight out of Zack, an' he wins an' loses a few battles down there while he's healin' up.

"It's a few years later Zack comes near crossin' the range, when he mixes with a fighter in Benton. The battle's Zack's from the start, till the other fellow cheats by drawin' a knife, an' slippin' it into Zack's flank he walks clean 'round him, leavin' Zack with nothin' holdin' him up but his backbone. His friends help him gather up the loose ends, and gettin' a doctor with a sackin' needle, he's soon patched up again.

"Another time Zack fights a feller all day. Of course they stop for drinks an' feed. There really ain't no hard feelins'; they're just tryin' to find out which is the best man. They'd a-been fightin' yet, but their eyes swelled shut at last an' they couldn't find one another.

"There was one town Zack was doubtful of, an' that was Bull Hook. In them days this burg held the pennant for fighters.

"Zack had been cookin' on the Teton roundup, an' when they break up that fall he jumps a train headed east. He's got quite a bankroll, and a friend stakes him to a quart that ain't grape juice. He's figurin' on winterin' in some of the towns along the road, so when the train stops at this town of Bull Hook, or Havre as they call it now, he steps off to get the air an' size up the citizens.

"As I was sayin', this town in the old days was the home of most of the fighters of the Northwest. Zack picks out the biggest, hardest one in sight, an' walkin' up friendly like, hands him one in the jaw with every pound he's got. With this the ball opens, but it don't last long, an' Zack's hit him everywhere when the big feller hollers 'enough.'

"Then the stranger wants to know what it's all about, and

asks Zack to introduce himself an' explain, just out of curiosity, what's his reason for tearin' into him. Zack tells him there's no hard feelin's an' it ain't no old grudge he's workin' off, but he kind of figured on winterin' in Bull Hook, an' hearin' they're all fighters there, he thinks this is the best way of introducin' himself.

"'I picked the biggest one among you,' says the Mormon. 'If I'd a-lose, I was goin' on to Chinook, but seein' I win, I'll winter with you.' An' he did.

"Although Zack's a natural scrapper, like many of his kind he has plenty of good traits, is good-hearted, an' I never knowed him to jump on a weakling; it was always a man who claimed to be a fighter, too. Zack belonged to his time, an' it was his kind and not the reformers that made Montana. These last came with the tumble-weed."

THAT story that Dad Lane tells the other night 'bout his compadre getting killed off, sure shows the Injun up," says "Squaw" Owens. "Injuns is born bushwhackers; they believe in killin' off their enemy an' ain't particular how it's done, but prefer gettin' him from cover, an' I notice some of their white brothers play the same way. You watch these old gun-fighters an' you'll see most of 'em likes a shade the start in a draw; there's many a man that's fell under the smoke of a forty-five—drawn from a sneak—that ain't lookin' when he got it.

"I've had plenty experience amongst Injuns, an' all the affection I got for 'em wouldn't make no love story, but with all their tricks an' treachery I call them a game people. It's their religion to die without a whimper; in olden times when a prisoner's took, there's no favors asked or given. He's up agin it. It's a sure case of cash in—skinned alive, cooked over a slow fire, or some such pleasant trail to the huntin'-ground—an' all Mister Prisoner does is to take his medicine without whinin'. If he makes any talk it's to tell ye you're a green hand at the business; of course he don't cuss none, he don't know how. That art belongs to civilized folks, but an Injun's got a string of names to call ye that'll do till something better comes along. They sure talk scandalous about you an' your relations.

"Talkin' about an Injun's nerve reminds me of an old buck I run onto on the Blackfoot Reserve a few years ago. I'm ridin' for the Flyin' O; this outfit's fillin' a beef contract, an' throwin' steers into the Agency near where we're holdin' the beef on Two Medicine, close-herdin'.

"There's an old Injun comes visitin' our camp, an' after he feeds once you can bet on him showin' up 'bout noon every day. If there's a place where an Injun makes a hand, it's helpin' a neighbor hide grub, an' they ain't particular about quality—it's quantity they want. Uncle Sam's Injuns average about one good meal a week; nobody's got to graze this way long till a tin plate loaded with beans looks like a Christmas dinner.

"This old buck takes a great likin' to me an' the chuck wagon, an' as I can talk some Blackfoot we get right sociable. I get this talk from a 'Live Dictionary' the year before, when I wintered up on Old Man's River; that is, I marry a Blood woman. When I say marry, I traded her pa two ponies an' a Winchester, an' in accordance with all Injun's law we're necked all right. Of course I furnish grub an' material to her relations for a tea dance to make the weddin' fashionable.

"But our married life ain't joyful—I sure kick on that cookin', for there ain't enough Injun in me to like it.

"Thinkin' to civilize her a little, I buy her a white woman's rig at McLeod, an' when she slips this on I'm damned if you can tell which way she's travelin'.

"We ain't been married a week till I've learned enough of the talk to call her all the names known to Blackfeet, an' by spring we can pull off nearly as good a quarrel as civilized folks in harness. When grass comes we separate; there's no divorce needed, as we're both willin', so we split the blankets; she pulls for camp, an' I drift south.

"But this old buck I started to tell ye about—Finger-That-Kills is his name—is all Injun from his moccasins up. If it ain't for his calico shirt an' leggin's an' clout bein' made of blanket instead of skin, he's dressed like he'd be a hundred years ago.

"The first day he shows up I notice he's shy three fingers on his right hand, leavin' nothin' but his thumb an' trigger finger.

Now he don't look to me like he's ever railroaded or worked in a sawmill, an' of course I'm curious to know who worked him over. So one day I'm layin' in the shade of my hoss on herd, when old Finger-That-Kills rides up on his little pinto whittledig for a visit. It's then I ask him how he gets trimmed up. He don't say nothin' for a long time, but goes to gazin' off on the prairie like he's lookin' for somethin'. Now folks that don't know Injuns 'ud think he don't hear me, but I heap savvy he's reachin' back in his history for the yarn I want.

"The only book he's got is these old prairies, but it's open to him an' he knows every leaf in her; I tell you, fellers, she sure holds good yarns for them that can read her.

"Finally he shakes out his black stone pipe, an' layin' her down, opens up on his yarn.

"'My cousin, it's a long way behind me,' says he, drawin' his crippled hand slow from his left, out in front of him an' back over his shoulder, which means in signs 'very long.'

A BLACKFOOT WOMAN

"'Forty times I've seen the snow come an' go since I took my first war-trail. I was then young an' my heart was strong.'

"Now I can't give it to you as flowery as this Injun does, 'cause these people are sure pretty with talk, but as I interpret it he's 'bout nineteen—the age the Reds begin lookin' for a mate—when he starts ridin' 'round on a painted pony an' puttin' in his time lookin' pretty. When a bunch of young squaws is down gettin' water, he accidentally rides through the creek, givin' them a chance to admire him. He's ablaze with paint an' feathers—to hear him tell it he's rigged out so it hurts your eyes to look at him, an' it ain't hard to imagine, 'cause I've seen young bucks stripped to the clout an' moccasins, painted till they're sure gaudy.

"Well, he finally sees the one he's lookin' for; she's as pretty as a painted wagon an' loves him right back. Now some folks think Injuns don't have love scrapes, but don't ever believe it. There's many a squaw that leaves camp with a rawhide under her blanket, an' next day she's found hangin' in a cottonwood—all because she can't get the buck she wants. An' the bucks are just as locoed in their way.

"Well, as I said before, Finger-That-Kills is sure warmed on this squaw; they're both willin', but he ain't got the price. He's shy on ponies, as her old dad's holdin' her for fifteen an' he's only got five, so it's a case of steal hosses or lose the girl.

"It's spring an' time for the Sun-Dance, so when that's pulled off he takes a hand an' goes through all right. Shortly after, there's a war-party starts for the Crow country, an' he's among 'em; there's fifteen, all afoot—an' travelin' light—stealin' parties generally goes this way. Each man's packin' his bundle of moccasins, dried meat, a rawhide rope an' weepons—mostly bows, as guns is scarce them days; the ones they've got is flintlocks that go off whenever they feel like it.

"They travel many sleeps with nothin' happenin' except runnin' low on meat, but that's nothin'—no Injun's supposed to get hungry on a war-trip. Finally they run clean out of pemmican, an' they're gettin' ga'nt an' wolfy. There's plenty of game, but they can't hunt, bein' afoot, an' it's pretty ticklish work disturbin' buffalo in the enemy's country. There's no tellin' what butte holds a red sentinel wrapped to the eyes in his robe. You can't see him, but he's there, still as a sleepin' snake. He don't need no bring-'em-close glasses; nature's give him a couple of beady blinkers that ain't wore none by readin', an' what they overlook ain't worth huntin' up.

"He sees the herd way yonder in the open; maybe there's a couple of bulls locked horns to one side, or one gougin' out a waller. The herd may be trailin' in to water, leavin' long strings of dust. These maneuvers don't excite him none, but let 'em start runnin', millin', or churnin', an' he's sure interested, for there ain't but one animal that'll cause these brown grass-eaters to act up that away— and that animal walks on hind legs an' ain't haired over.

"This lookout heap savvys, an' you can bet he ain't slow at signalin'. He's got several ways of telegraphin', accordin' to time an' weather. If the sun's right, it's a lookin' glass; if it's too windy for smoke, it's a blanket or robe, an' at night, a fire. An' it's sur- prisin' how quick he'll change that quiet, peaceful scene. Before you know it the country's swarmin' with painted, feathered hair- hunters, an' hell's poppin'. Of course the Blackfeet know all this an' they're mighty cautious.

"They're nearin' the Crow country, travelin' nights, 'mostly. One mornin' just breakin' day, Finger-That-Kills is sneakin' along ahead of his party—kind of advance scout. He's sure hungry, his belt's cinched to its last hole, an' he can't think of nothin' but eatin', when of a sudden he stumbles right onto a big bull. This old buffalo's got three wolves around him; he's hamstrung an' down behind, but whirlin' 'round an' makin' a good stand-off with his horns. When Mister Injun walks up, these wolves go slinkin' off, makin' faces at him; they don't like bein' busted in on at meal-times.

"With a couple of arrows Finger-That-Kills finishes the bull, but before touchin' the meat, holdin' up his hands, he thanks the sun, who's just peepin' over the sky-line. You may not know it, but all Injuns is great people to give thanks to their God.

"Then he cuts in an' gets the liver; Redskins are sure fond of this, raw an' warm. He's so busy fillin' up that he gets careless; there's a flock of sage hens comes sailin' over that disturbs his meal, an' the next thing he knows three Injuns comes yelpin' down on him, quirtin' their ponies at every jump.

"Now there's a bunch of cottonwoods not far from where he's sittin' that looks mighty handy, so he hits the breeze, not runnin' straight, but sidewindin', duckin', an' dodgin' like a grouse-hen tollin' ye from her nest.

"He's a hard mark, but he ain't made three of these curves till a trade ball goes plowin' up under his scalp an' he turns over on his face as dead as he'll ever be, for a minute. When he comes to, the strangers are down off their ponies, jokin' an' laughin'. Of course Finger-That-Kills don't see the humor; he's playin' dead for all there's in it. They're Gros Ventres—he knows this by the few words he savvys of their guttural tongue. He feels the hand of his enemy twisted in his scalp-lock, an' it ain't no guess with him that he'll be losing some hair shortly. He is layin' face down, his right hand's stretched out along the ground, his left doubled under him. Bein' a dandy an' a leader of fashion, he wears jewelry regardless, an' his hands are loaded to the knuckles with brass trade rings.

"The Gros Ventre's eye for finery is caught by this glitter, an' droppin' the hair he reaches for the jeweled hand, first tryin' to slip the rings. But they're tight, so takin' his knife he begins hackin' the fingers off.

"Now's when Finger-That-Kills comes in with that Injun nerve I'm tellin' you about. He lays there not movin' a muscle, an' all the comfort he gets is gnawin' a branch of sage brush his head's layin' in, while this operation is goin' on.

"The Gros Ventre's sawin' away on his middle finger when

"THE GROS VENTRE BEGINS HACKIN' THE FINGERS OFF"

Mister Blackfoot hears the welcome yelpin' of his party comin' up on the back trail.

"The minute these Big Bellies see they're outnumbered, they crawl their ponies an' bust the breeze; havin' hosses the best of it, they make a clean get-away. Finger-That-Kills is glad he's livin' an's got his hair, but he's sure sore 'bout losin' those rings.

"This little trouble don't stop the Blackfeet. They reach the Crows all right, an' come back with two hundred stolen ponies.

"Of course Finger-That-Kills gets his squaw all right, but this don't end his love scrapes, for an Injun with one wire is a tolerable poor husband. These people set no limit to matrimony, an' count wealth by squaws an' hosses.

"'How does it feel,' says I, 'when that Gros Ventre's trimmin' you?'

"'The Big Belly's lazy; his knife's dull—very dull. The dog-eater's foolish like a squaw when he leaves me this,' says he, smilin' an' holdin' up his lone finger. 'For this one has killed two Big Bellies for every one of his dead brothers, an' their scalps have long dried in the lodge of the Finger-That-Kills.'"

DOG EATER

A MAN that ain't never been hungry can't tell nobody what's good to eat," says Rawhide Rawlins. "I eat raw sow bosom and frozen biscuit when it tasted like a Christmas dinner.

"Bill Gurd tells me he's caught one time. He's been ridin' since daybreak and ain't had a bite. It's plumb dark when he hits a breed's camp. This old breed shakes hands and tells Bill he's welcome, so after strippin' his saddle and hobblin' his hoss, he steps into the shack. Being wolf hungry, he notices the old woman's cooking bannocks at the mud fire. Tired and hungry like Bill is, the warmth and the smell of grub makes this cottonwood shack, that ain't much more than a windbreak, look like a palace.

"'Tain't long till the old woman hands him a tin plate loaded with stew and bannocks, with hot tea for a chaser. He don't know what kind of meat it is but he's too much of a gentleman to ask. So he don't look a gift hoss in the mouth. After he fills up, while he's smokin', the old man spreads down some blankets and Bill beds down.

"Next mornin' he gets the same for breakfast. Not being so hungry, he's more curious, but don't ask no questions. On the way out to catch his hoss he gets an answer. A little ways from the cabin, he passes a fresh dog hide pegged down on the ground. It's like seeing the hole-card—it's no gamble what that stew was made of, but it was good and Bill held it.

"I knowed another fellow one time that was called Dog Eatin' Jack. I never knowed how he got his name that's hung to him, till I camp with him. This old boy is a prospector and goes gopherin' 'round the hills, hopin' he'll find something.

"I'm huntin' hosses one spring and ain't found nothing but tracks. I'm up on the Lodgepole in the foothills; it's sundown and my hoss has went lame. We're limping along slow when I sight a couple of hobbled cayuses in a beaver meadow. One of these hosses is wearing a Diamond G iron, the other's a Quarter-Circle-Block hoss. They're both old cow ponies. I soon locate their owner's camp —it's a lean-to in the edge of the timber.

"While I'm lookin' over the layout, here comes the owner. It's the Dog Eater. After we shake hands I unsaddle and stake out my tired hoss. When we're filled up on the best he's got—which is beans, bacon, and frying pan bread, which is good filling for hungry men—we're sittin' smokin', and it's then I ask him if he ever lived with Injuns.

"'You're thinkin',' says he, 'about my name. It does sound like Injun, but they don't hang it on me. It happens about ten winters ago. I'm 'way back in the Diamond range; I've throwed my hosses about ten mile out in the foothills where there's good feed and less snow. I build a lean-to, a good one, and me and my dog settles down. There's some beaver here and I got out a line of traps and figger on winterin' here. Ain't got much grub, but there's lots of game in the hills and my old needle gun will get what the traps won't.

"'Snow comes early and lots of it. About three days after the storm I step on a loose boulder and sprain my ankle. This puts me plumb out; I can't more than keep my fire alive. All the time I'm running short of grub. I eat a couple of skinned beaver I'd throwed away one day. My old dog brings in a snowshoe rabbit to camp and maybe you don't think he's welcome. I cut in two with him but manlike, I give him the front end. That's the last we got.

"'Old Friendship—that's the dog's name—goes out every day, but he don't get nothing and I know he ain't cheating—he's too holler in the flanks. After about four days of living on thoughts,

Friendship starts watchin' like he's afraid. He thinks maybe I'll put him in the pot, but he sizes me up wrong. If I'd do that, I hope I choke to death.

"'The sixth day I'm sizin' him up. He's laying near the fire. He's a hound with a long meaty tail. Says I to myself, 'Oxtail soup! What's the matter with dog tail?' He don't use it for nothing but sign talk, but it's like cutting the hands off a dummy. But the eighth day, with hunger and pain in my ankle, I plumb locoed and I can't get that dog's tail out of my mind. So, a little before noon I slip up on him, while he's sleeping, with the ax. In a second it's all over, Friendship goes yelpin' into the woods and I am sobbin' like a kid, with his tail in my hand.

"'The water is already boiling in the pot, an' as soon as I singe the hair off it's in the pot. I turned a couple of flour sacks inside out and dropped them in and there's enough flour to thicken

"PRIENDSHIP GOES YELPIN' INTO THE WOODS"

the soup. It's about dark. I fill up, and if it weren't for thinkin' it would have been good. I could have eat it all but I held out over half for Friendship, in case he come back.

"'It must be midnight when he pushes into the blankets with me. I take him in my arms. He's as cold as a dead snake, and while I'm holdin' him tight I'm crying like a baby. After he warms up a little, I get up and throw some wood on the fire and call Friendship to the pot. He eats every bit of it. He don't seem to recognize it. If he does, being a dog, he forgives.

"'We go back to the blankets. It's just breaking day when he slides out, whinin' and sniffin' the air with his ears cocked and his bloody stub wobblin'. I look the way he's pointin', and not twenty-five yards from the lean-to stands a big elk. There's a fine snow fallin'; the wind's right for us. I ain't a second gettin' my old needle gun, but I'm playin' safe—I'm coming Injun on him. I use my ram-rod for a rest. When old needle speaks, the bull turns over—his neck's broken. 'Tain't long till we both get to that bull and we're both eatin' raw, warm liver. I've seen Injuns do this but I never thought I was that much wolf, but it was sure good that morning.

"'He's a big seven-point bull—old and pretty tough, but me and Friendship was looking for quantity, not quality, and we got it. That meat lasted till we got out.'

"'What became of Friendship?' says I.

"'He died two years ago,' says Jack. 'But he died fat.'"

MOST folks don't bank much on squaw-men, but I've seen some mighty good ones doubled up with she-Injuns," says Dad Lane. "Ain't you, Owens?"

"I told you my short experience with that Blood woman; I wasn't a successful Injun, but the comin' of white women to the country's made big changes; men's got finicky about matin'. I guess if I'd come to the country earlier, squaws would a-looked good enough, an' if there wasn't nothin' but Injun women, it's a cinch that all married men would be wearin' moccasins. There's a whole lot of difference livin' with Injuns now an' when the buffalo were thick; the savages owned the country then.

"When I'm ridin' line for the H-half-H, my camp's on the border of the Piegan Reserve. Of course I gets lots of visits from my red brothers. Among 'em is an old squaw-man named Lindsay. He's white all right, but you'd have to be a good guesser to call the turn. Livin' so long with Injuns, he's got all their ways an' looks. Can't talk without usin' his hands. His white hair's down over his shoulder an' his wrinkled face is hairless. By the holes punched in his ears I know he's wore rings sometimes. He packs a medicine-bag, all same savage.

"From his looks an' the dates he gives me, he's crowdin' eighty winters. This old boy could string the best war and buffalo yarns I ever heard. It's like readin' a romance; any time he calls I'm sure of a good yarn.

"I remember one day we're sittin' outside the shack, clear of the eaves. There's a Chinook blowing an' the roof's drippin' like it's rainin'. It's mighty pleasant in the sun out of the wind. This old breeze is cuttin' the snow off the hills in a way that's a blessin' to cows an' cowmen. The country's been hid for six weeks, an' if the Chinook hadn't come, cowmen would needed skinnin'-knives instead of brandin'-irons.

"As I said before, we're sittin' outside enjoyin' the change; the white Injun's smokin' his mixture of willow bark an' tobacco, while I'm sizin' him up, an' somehow I can't help but pity him. Here's an old man as white as I am. No doubt he's been a great man with these savages, but he's nothin' or nobody to his own blood or color. While I'm thinkin' about him in this way he starts mumblin' to himself in Injun. I don't savvy only part of it, so I ask him what it's all about. He says he's talkin' to the sun; he's thankin' him for the warm wind that melts the snow.

"'Don't you believe in God?' says I.

"'Yes,' says he.

"'What kind of a one?'

"'That one,' says he, pintin' with his staff to the sun. 'The one I can see an' have watched work for many years. He gathers the clouds an' makes it rain; then warms the ground an' the grass turns green. When it's time he dries it yellow, makin' it good winter feed for grass-eaters.

"'Again, when he's mad, my people say he drives the rain away, dryin' up the streams an' water-holes. If it wasn't for him there couldn't nothin' or nobody live. Do you wonder that we pray him to be good an' thank him when he is? I'm all Injun but my hide; their God's my God, an' I don't ask for no better.'

"'However did you come to throw in with these savages in the start-off?' says I.

"'Well, boys, I'll tell you how it happened,' says he, signin' for a match, an' lightin' up fresh, he starts off.

"'There used to be lots of white Injuns like me—what you'd call squaw-men, but I've outlived the most of 'em. Some got civilized, throwed away their red women an' took white ones, but I've been too long in the Piegan camp to change, an', nearin' the end o' the road like I am, I guess I'll finish with the red ones.

"'It's the women that make the men in this world, I heard an educated feller say once, an' it's the truth that, if a man's goin' to hell or heaven, if you look in the trail ahead of him you'll find a track the same shape as his, only smaller; it's a woman's track. She's always ahead, right or wrong, tollin' him on. In animals, the same as humans, the female leads. That ain't the exact words this educated man uses, but it's as near as I can interpret, an' it's the truth. If you ever run buffalo, you'll notice the cow-meats in the lead. With wild hosses the stallion goes herdin' them along, snakin' an' bowin' his neck, with his tail flagged. From looks you'd call him chief, but the mares lead to the water-hole they've picked out. An' I believe, if all women were squaws, the whites would be wearin' clouts to-day.

"'In early times when white men mixed with Injuns away from their own kind, these wild women in their paint an' beads looked mighty enticin', but to stand in with a squaw you had to turn Injun. She'd ask were your relations all dead that you cut your hair? or was you afraid the enemy'd get a hold an' lift it?— at the same time givin' you the sign for raisin' the scalp. The white man, if he liked the squaw, wouldn't stand this joshin' long till he throwed the shears away, an' by the time the hair reached his shoulders he could live without salt. He ain't long forgettin' civilization. Livin' with Nature an' her people this way, he goes backwards till he's a raw man, without any flavorin'. In grade, he's a notch or two above a wolf, follerin' the herds for his meat the same as his wild dog-brother. But, boy, I started to tell you about myself.'

"An' this is about the way he strings it to me.

"He's born in St. Louis, at that time the outfittin'-place for all fur trade south of the British line. His first remembrance, when he's a youngster, is seein' traders in from their far-off, unknown country. These long-haired fellers, some in fringed buckskin, others in bright-colored blanket-clothes, strike the kid's fancy. There's Frenchmen an' Breeds that's come down in boats loaded with buffalo an' beaver hides, from the upper Missouri. From the Southwest comes the Spanish an' Mexican traders, their hundreds of pack-mules loaded with pelts. These men are still more gaudy, with silver braid an' buttons from their broad sombreros to their six-inch rowels, all wearin' bright-colored sashes an' serapis. Sometimes

"FROM THE SOUTHWEST COMES SPANISH AN'
MEXICAN TRADERS"

a band of Pawnees would drift in from the plains, their faces painted an' heads shaved, barrin' the scalplock.

"All these sights make this romantic kid restless, an' it wouldn't take much to make him break away. So one day a tannin' he gets from his step-dad gives him all the excuse he needs, an' bustin' home ties, he quits the village as fast as his small feet an' shanks will pack him. Follerin' the Mississippi he's mighty leg-weary an' hungry next mornin' when he meets up with Pierre Chouteau's cordellers or boatmen. He tells 'em his story between whimpers an' tears, an' these big-hearted river travelers feed him an' take him in.

"They're about the mouth of the Missouri when he overtakes 'em, towin' north with goods for the Upper Missouri trade. This trip ain't no picnic, but bein' a strong, healthy kid, he enjoys it. They pass the dirt-lodge towns of the Mandans an' Rickarees, that look like overgrown anthills, where the Injuns come to meet 'em in bowl-shaped bull-boats, made of green buffalo hide stretched on willers. Many times they're stopped by herds of buffalo crossin' the river. It's pretty smooth for the kid, chorin' around an' herdin' hosses for the post, till one day he falls asleep an' a war-party of Crows drop down an' get about half of 'em. This makes the chief of the post hostile, an' he has Lindsay licked. This old man tells me that the chiefs of tradin'-posts made their own laws, an' when you broke one you had a floggin' comin'. Sometimes men were shot or hung, accordin' to how serious the break was. The lickin' he gets is too much for him, so he busts out an' makes a get-away.

"There's about a hundred lodges of Piegans pullin' north, camped two mile above the post. He finds out these Injuns will break camp about daybreak. It's gettin' gray when he clears the stockade. On reachin' the camp-ground he's mighty disappointed in findin' nothin' but the dead ashes of their fires. He's afraid to go back to the post, an' the Missouri lays between him an' the

Injuns, so bein' desperate, he strips his garments an' takes the water. Before startin' he ties his clothes in a pack on his shoulders.

"The water's low an' don't require much swimmin', but nearin' the bank on the fur side, an undercurrent catches him an' he loses his gun. This old flintlock is mighty dear to him, but it's a case of lighten up or go under, so he loosens his holt, hittin' the shore with nothin' but a wet powder-horn an' a skinnin'-knife. The draggin' of hundreds of travois an' lodge poles makes a trail as easy to foller as a wagon road. About noon he reaches the rear guard. In them days Injuns traveled, when in dangerous country, with advance, flank, an' rear guard, their squaws, children, an' loose ponies in the centre. The Piegans, bein' in the Sioux country, ain't takin' no chances.

"When he meets up with the rear guard they're down off their ponies, figurin' on a smoke, but they've lost the steel an' there don't happen to be a flintlock gun in this bunch. They're tryin' hard to get a light by hackin' an old iron trade knife agin the flint. When Lindsay looms up, Injun-like, they don't hardly notice him. These months around the post, he's picked up considerable hand-talk, so signs 'em he'll light their pipe. One old pock-marked buck, that's holdin' the pipe an' seems to be chief, says, 'The boy is foolish, if he has no steel, to talk to old men.'

"Lindsay don't make no back talk, but, walkin' up to the old man, signs him to hold the bowl up; that the sun will make smoke. Then, reachin' in his pouch, he pulls a sun-glass. As I says before, it's about noon an' the sun's well up. It's one of them warm fall days, not a cloud in the sky; this makes it easy for Lindsay, so holdin' the glass above the bowl an' movin' her up an' down till he gets the focus, an' holdin' her steady, it's not long before the little bright light down in the bowl sends up a fine curl of smoke. The old Injun, seein' this, takes a long draw, an' when they all see the smoke roll from the old chief's nostrils they're plenty surprised, but don't

"PULLIN' MY GUN, I EMPTY HER IN THE AIR."

VERS MAKE SECRET

"I'M SCAREDER OF HIM THAN I AM OF THE INJUNS."

TORS

BLACKFEET

show it none; 'tain't Injun nature. You could take one of these savages up to the Missouri River an' by a wave of your hand stop the flow an' back her up a mile; an' if he didn't want to, he wouldn't change expression; he wouldn't even look interested. His old insides might be boilin' with astonishment, but you'd never know it. On these people it don't show through the hide.

"When they get through passin' the pipe, they all fork their ponies, an' the old Injun signs the kid to crawl up behind him on his pony. He's pretty leg-weary an' don't wait for no second invite, so rides double the rest of the way with the old man. By the time they reach camp the news is spread 'round about the medicine-boy that lights the pipe with the sun. He can hardly eat his supper for Injuns crowdin' around takin' a peek at him. The young women look at him, the old hags kiss him, an' the mothers rub their pa- pooses on his breast to get his medicine. Lindsay takes it all good- humored, barrin' the old ladies kissin' him, which he says don't mix well with his supper. That night Lindsay tells the old man how the trader treated him an' begs not to be sent back.

"This old Injun, Wounded Hoss is his name, is chief of the band. He tells the boy he'll not be sent back an' there's no danger of the trader follerin' him, for a white man that follers a Piegan those days, unless he's lookin' for trouble, is plumb silly.

"'The grass has grown twice since my two sons were killed by the Sioux,' says the old chief; 'my heart is on the ground; I am lonesome, but since the sun has sent you, it is good. I will adopt you as my boy. I am old an' my muscles are tired—very tired. My lodge is yours till you're old enough to take a woman. I have plenty ponies, an' among them good buffalo hosses. You shall ride them, an' bring meat an' robes to my women. Child of the Sun, it is good.' An' after that, until Lindsay won his war-name, he was known as 'Child of the Sun.'

"Next day his new father gives him a bow an' otter-skin quiver, filled with steel-pointed arrows. This bow is of fine make, choke-cherry wood, wrapped with sinew. With this rig, mounted on a fine pinto, this kid wouldn't trade places with the President.

"The first few days there ain't nothin' happens; Lindsay rides along with the bunch, learnin' to handle the bow. This ain't no easy trick, for though a bow with a Injun behind it's a nasty weapon, with a green hand it's mighty near harmless. It takes an expert to pull an arrow back to the head, an' it's several years before Lindsay can get the knack an' can drive his arrow to the feathers. The Injun pulls his string with three an' sometimes four fingers, with all his strength, an' by gettin' back of the ribs, an' aimin' forward, he'll drive his arrow plumb to the lungs an' sometimes clean through a buffalo.

"Lindsay's enjoyin' the life fine, barrin' his everlastin' longin' for salt an' sugar. He craves it all day an' dreams of it nights, an' it's months before he's plumb weaned.

"About the fourth evenin' some scouts ride in with news of a big herd they've located a short ride north of 'em, so all hands pre-pare for a surround next day. The kid's so excited he don't sleep much. All night long he can hear the tom-tom of the medicine-man. It's just breakin' day when he wakes. Everybody an' the dogs are up. Quittin' the pile of robes he throws the lodge door aside. The ponies are among the lodges; squaws an' bucks are all busy pickin' out their mounts. From the fires in front of the lodges he can smell meat cookin'. Lookin' around he spies his foster father wrapped to his eyes in his robes. He don't recognize him in the dim light till he speaks.

"'My son, bring your rope an' foller me,' says Wounded Hoss.

"Gettin' his rawhide, Lindsay follers the old man among the ponies, an' after two or three throws, gets his loop over a black pinto that is pointed out to him as his buffalo hoss.

"While they're eatin', one of the kid's foster mothers leads up

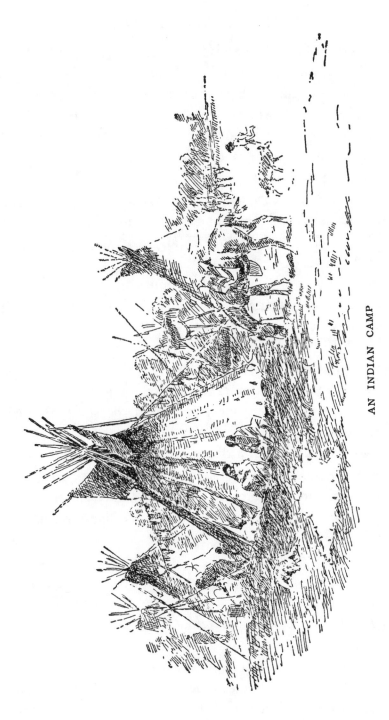

AN INDIAN CAMP

141

three more ponies. One of these is for Wounded Hoss; the other for his adopted boy. Injuns generally led their buffalo hosses to the runnin' ground, an' that's what these extra mounts is for. In them days buffalo hosses was worth plenty of robes. This animal had to be sure-footed, long-winded, an' quick as a cat. It's no bench of a hoss that'll lay alongside of a buffalo cow, while you're droppin' arrows or lead in her. He's got to be a dodger, all the same cow-hoss, 'cause a wounded cow's liable to get ringy or on the fight, an' when she does, she's mighty handy with them black horns. An Injun's sure proud of his buffalo hoss, an' this animal gets the best a savage can give it. Old Lindsay tells me, in winters, when it's a bad storm, he's seen 'em put the ponies in the lodges an' the squaws would bring grass that they cut with their knives or a kind of hoe that they had for that purpose.

"This white Injun tells me that if he lives a thousand years, he'll never forget that day. Just this bunch of riders is a sight worth seein'. There's about two hundred bucks, youngsters an' all, an' ponies—well, there ain't no color known to hossflesh that ain't there. Some of 'em's painted till you couldn't tell what shade of hide they wear. Each buck's ridin' an ordinary-lookin' cayuse, but the one he's leadin', or's got a light boy ridin', is sure gay an' gaudy, with tail an' foretop tied up an' decked with feathers. Maybe he's got a medicine-bag hangin' in his mane to make him strong an' lucky. Paint's smeared regardless, an' there's pictures all over him.

"Barrin' some old coffee-cooler mumblin' a prayer, or a pony clearin' his nostrils, these riders are joggin' along pretty near as noiseless as a band of ghosts. Barefoot ponies on well-grassed sod travel mighty silent, an' the savages ain't doin' no talkin' except with their hands. This is where sign-talk comes in mighty handy. In quiet weather the mumble of a dozen men will travel for miles, but with hand-talk a thousand Injuns might be within gunshot, an' you'd never know it. Buffalo, like most four-footed animals, are wind-readers, but there ain't nothin' the matter with their hearin', so, after gettin' the wind right, Mr. Injun makes a sneak, an' there ain't nobody capable of givin' him lessons in the art of hidin' or sneakin'. It's been proved; for years they've played 'I spy' with Uncle Sam, an' most of the time Uncle's been 'It.'

"They ain't gone four miles when a scout looms up on a butte an' signs with his robe. This signal causes them all to spread out an' every Injun slides from his pony an' starts backin' out of his cowskin shirt an' skinnin' his leggin's. 'Tain't a minute till they're all stripped to the clout an' moccasins, forkin' their ponies naked like themselves, barrin' two half hitches of rawhide on the lower jaw. That sign means that the herd is in sight an' close. When they're all mounted, the scout on the butte swings his robe a couple of times around his head an' drops it. Before it hits the ground every pony's runnin', with a red rider quirtin' him down the hind leg, leavin' little curls of dust in the yellow grass behind him. At the top of the ridge the herd shows—a couple of thousand, all spread out grazin'. But seein' these red hunters pilin' down on 'em, their heads leave the grass. One look's a plenty, an' with tails straightened, they start lumberin' together. It ain't long till they've bunched, millin' an' churnin', all same spotted cattle.

"When Lindsay gets to 'em, the dust's rollin' so he just gets a glimpse now an' again of his naked brothers emptyin' their quivers. He notices Mr. Injun pull five or six arrows at a draw, holdin' the extras in his mouth an' bow-hand, an' the way he's got of turnin' 'em loose don't trouble him none. Above the rumble an' gruntin' of these animals, he faintly hears now an' agin the reports of a fuke, or sawed-off flintlock, or the quick, sharp yelp of the Injun, as he sends his arrow home. Barrin' this, it's all dust an' rumblin'. Lindsay singles out a cow for his meat. The dodgin' of his pony mighty near unloads him, but by hookin' his toe under the fore leg, Injun fashion, he manages to keep his hoss under him. The kid gets the cow all right, but he tells me she resembles a porcupine; her hide's bristlin' with arrows when she lays down. After the run's over, they've made a killin' of about three hundred. While the squaws are skinnin', Lindsay lunches on raw liver, like any other Injun. Looks like this short run has turned him savage.

"'My boy,' says Lindsay, finishin' up his yarn, openin' an' shuttin' his hands like an Injun—I savvy he's countin' winters—'that's been sixty-five years ago as near as I can figure. I run buffalo till the whites cleaned 'em out, but that's the day I turned Injun, an' I ain't cut my hair since.'"

"I TURNED INJUN AN' I AIN'T CUT MY HAIR SINCE"

BROKE BUFFALO

THERE used to be a man on the Yellerstone," says Raw-hide Rawlins, "that catches a pair of yearling buffalo. He handles them hump-back cows till they're plumb gentle—they hang around the ranch like any other cows.

"One day he decides to put them in the yoke. That bump fits back of the yoke and in all ways they are built for work. But he finds looks are deceivin' when he rigs a pole on a pair of old hind wheels, making a kind of cart—it's no sulky, 'tain't built for speed, but that's what it's used for. They ain't hard to yoke. He's whacked bulls and skinned mules, but when he gets up behind this team he can't find no team talk the pair savvies. He's usin' rope reins but they might as well be thread—he couldn't bend their necks with a canthook.

"Finally, they start. Maybe these hump-backs know where they's going, but this driver ain't got no idea. 'Tain't long till he's in a country he ain't never saw, but judgin' from the sun he's going south, an' both wheels are smoking. They run over a jackrabbit and pass a band of antelope that's doing their damdest. It's after-noon when the hurry-up party hits a rut that breaks the driver's hold and he lands in a patch of buck brush. He's dam' glad of it—

145

he's plumb tired holdin'. He don't know how far they went, but don't get home till noon next day. About a week later his team shows up at the corral—they're still packing the yoke. They don't show no signs of being jaded.

"Next spring a neighbor talks him into breaking sod with them. He gets to thinkin' this over, and knowin' they got the power he hooks them onto a plow. This time he heads them north, but this direction suits them. It's springtime and they don't mind going north. He's got his plow sunk to the beam—it slows their gait some but he can't turn them. They started north and that's where they's going. Streams don't stop them, and when he quits the handles they's still plowing north.

"He finds out that these animals travel north in the spring and south in the fall. If he could find a country with seasons no longer than this field, they'd do good for a driving team. If he was fixed so he could spend his winters in Mexico and his summers in Canada, they'd just be the thing. He hears from them through a friend late that summer—they're north of the Teton, plowing south."

"MAYBE THESE HUMP-BACKS KNOW WHERE THEY'S GOIN, BUT THE DRIVER AIN'T GOT NO IDEA"

THE conversation among the group at the end of the bar had turned to the subject of sudden death, when Rawhide Rawlins cuts in. "Several times in my life I've been close to the cash in," he says, "but about the nearest I ever come to crossin' the big range is a few years ago, before I move to Montana. This is down in California, an' there's a friend with me at the time—I ain't givin' his name, but we'll call him Bill Roslin. His father's a Chicago millionaire.

"Bill crosses over, and the reason I don't tell his right name is because his folks never know what kind of an end Bill meets. It seems he's out West for his parents' health, they remainin' in the East, an' it appears they never get the facts in the case. They believe to-day that their lovin' son quit this life in bed, with a preacher hangin' over him an' a doctor takin' the pulse count. The truth is there wasn't no one with him at the finish but me an' a team of hosses, an' the hosses take the long trail with him, leavin' me in the only travelin' cemetery I've ever seen.

"The way this incident starts, we are leanin' over the mahogany in a joint in Los Gatos, after a big night together. As we're both hoss lovers, we're givin' this subject a lot of our conversation, and finally Bill suggests that a buggy ride would be a good thing, as we're feelin' the need of some fresh air. We leave this joy parlor arm-in-arm and visit a friend of mine who owns a livery stable. I tell him what we're after, and he gives us the best he's got—a span of bays bred in the purple, and as good as any roadsters in California.

"For fear of losin' any of this joyful feelin' we've accumulated

147

we're heeled with a quart of corn juice, which we're partakin' of free and reg'lar as we spin along one of them good California roads with our hosses up and comin'. Bill keeps tellin' me how fancy he is with the reins, not forgettin' to criticise my drivin', for he's reached the stage where he's gettin' argumentative. From the line of talk he hands out I've got my doubts as to how much he knows about hoss flesh, but I'm not disputin' him any, for the whole world right now looks so beautiful to me that there's no chance for an argument on any subject from religion or Teddy Roosevelt to the best brand of red-eye. I want to sing, and do warble for awhile, but Bill ain't got no musical ear, and he claims the noise I'm makin' is frettin' the team and drivin' all the birds out of the country. From feelin' musical I begin to get sleepy, and the last I remember I'm dozin' off. I recollect Bill reachin' for the reins, and the next I know I've a vague notion I'm in an airship and can see clear to the Mexican line. I'm wonderin' where I changed cars when the light goes out.

"When I wake up I'm layin' with my feet higher than my head, and my eyes open slowly on a big marble tombstone with the letterin':

OUR LOVED ONE AT REST.
JOINED THE ANGELS
JUNE 30, 1911.

"I think to myself, I may be their 'loved one,' but they're liars when they say I'm at rest. There ain't a place on me that don't ache; even my hair is sore to the touch.

"I start figurin' from the date on the stone how long I've been dead, but my brain won't work and I give it up. While I'm wonderin' whether I'll have to make a squarin' talk with Peter, the gate-man, I hear the puff of a switch engine somewhere close by.

"'Since when,' thinks I, 'did they get a railroad built through here?' But the thirst I've got makes me think maybe I've took the southern route, and perhaps they're haulin' coal.

"'What the hell you doin' here?' breaks in a voice, and it ain't no angel talkin', so I realize that I'm in the same old world. Lookin' over the tombstone, sizin' me up, is the toughest lookin' brakie I ever see.

"'Where am I?' I inquire without movin'.

"He gives me the name of the burg, but it's a camp I never heard of.

"'If you'll lead me to a thirst parlor,' I says, 'I'll buy somethin' and you're in on it.'

"'You're on, Bo,' says he.

"Then, sittin' up and lookin' around, I discover I'm on a flat car loaded to the rims with tombstones, and I'm layin' in front of the biggest one in the lot. Although it nearly kills me to move, I scramble to the ground, and the brakie pilots me to a little joint across the tracks. There's nobody in there but the bartender and the flies, and this toddy mixer is busy readin' a newspaper. Throwin' my silver on the bar, I tell him to get in. It's pretty bad booze, but it helps bring me back to life. The bartender's sociable, and after I buy a couple of rounds for the three of us, pickin' up the paper again he says, 'Quite a killin' across the state.'

"'What killin'?' says I.

"'Some feller runs a team into a freight that's slidin' down a grade about three hundred miles south of here,' says the barkeep. 'Smashes himself and the team into chunks.'

"'I'll bet that's Bill Roslin,' I says. 'Seems to me I was buggy-ridin' with him some time this year. Judgin' from where I find myself this mornin', I was with him at the cash in.'

"'What do you think of that?' the brakie asks the bartender, tappin' his forehead.

"'Turn over, you're layin' on your back,' says the bartender.

'That smash-up happens a day's ride from here. Wait a minute, though,' he goes on. 'It does say here that there's a feller with him that they can't locate.'

"'Well, that's me,' says I.

"I find out later that Roslin tries to cut a freight in two with this team, killin' himself and both hosses. That's when I land among these grave ornaments and take a ride in a movin' cemetery."

A COW PONY

I DIDN'T go to the stockmen's meet at Miles, myself," says Rawhide Rawlins, "but Teddy Blue tells me about it, an' as the strongest thing he used as a joy bringer is a maple-nut sunday mixed by a lady bartender, I guess his sight is pretty clear.

"Teddy has attended a lot of these gatherings in years gone by, but always before those rock-bass eyes of his was dimmed by cow-swallows of Miles City home-made liquid fire, so he's mostly numb an' unconscious of what's goin' on after the first few hours.

"This time Teddy's a little nervous an' keeps his hat brim pretty well down over his eyes for the first few hours he's there, as he's not sure whether he'll be recognized by the man who was sheriff at Miles some years back an' wanted Teddy to take room an' board with him for a few months for shootin' up a canary bird in a place where Teddy an' a few of his friends are pullin' a concert. Ted claims this canary insulted him several times before he gets ringy by breakin' in with his ditty while Ted's singin' 'The Texas Ranger.'

"When Teddy leaves town that time, his hoss wonders at the hurry they're in, an' when they reach the high ground Ted looks back and sees there's still a string of dust in Milestown that ain't had time to settle since his hoss's feet tore it loose. He plays in luck, for the sheriff, knowin' Ted's from Texas, goes south, while Ted's headin' for the north pole. He's just toppin' the hill out of Miles when he runs down a jackrabbit that gets in his way. Teddy says he never thought a canary bird would have so many friends.

"So he feels easier at this meeting when he finds the sheriff an' all the canary's friends have either cashed in or left the country.

"Although Montana's gone dry, this special train from the north loaded with cowmen and flockminders don't seem to feel the drouth none, and Miles City itself acts cheerful under the affliction. Teddy, though he ain't drinkin' nothin' these days, admits to me on the quiet that just the little he inhales from his heavy-breathin' friends has him singin' 'The Dyin' Cowboy.' He figures the ginger ale and root beer they're throwin' into 'em must have got to workin' in the bottles a little, judgin' from the cheerful effect it has.

"There's another train from Helena, the headquarters for the law-makers, that's filled with a bunch that acts as care-free as if they'd forgot there's such a thing as an attorney-general in their camp. They overlooked bringin' any root beer with them, so they had to fall back on stuff they was used to. Teddy looked into one of the Helena cars, he says, and what he sees through the smoke reminds him of Butte in the days of licensed gamblin'. He's told they're only playin' a few harmless games like 'Old Maid,' so he figures they just have the chips lyin' around to make them feel at home. He says he can see one banker has plumb forgot how to play cards, for he notices him slip an ace off the bottom. Ted says the friendly and trustful feelin' among this Helena crowd is fine to see. One time during daylight they pass through a tunnel, an' strikin' a match, Teddy sees every man at the table he's watchin' leanin' forward all spread out over his chips. They was undoubtedly afraid they might jolt into another train and spill the chips around, an' of course it would be a job pickin' 'em up off the floor.

"There's one sport in the Fergus County bunch that was raised on the range, that for size and weight would take the prize at the state fair in the bull show, but he ain't wearin' any ribbons when Teddy looks at him.

"Another gent from the upper Sun River country, also born on the range an' raised in the saddle, ain't no baby in build. He's had a hoss under him so long that his legs is kind of warped, an' when he sits in one of the chairs they have these days in front of the root beer bars, he straddles it instead of sittin' like a human. This feller, like Teddy, ain't usin' nothin' stronger than the law allows now, but in ₁ld days he was no stranger to corn juice or any of the other beverages that brought cheer and pleasure to the life of a cowpuncher. At the stock meetin's he used to attend, all the speakin' he listened to was done in front of a bar.

"One of the oldest cow owners in the bunch, whose front name's Bill and who in years past was known all over Montana, does most of his ridin' in an automobile these days. Bill's in the bankin' business now an' you might think he's cold-blooded, but I know different. To sick folks he's almost motherly. One time in the Lake Basin country Bill's trailin' the F beef south, an' he's on ahead lookin' for water when he runs onto a sheepherder that's lyin' on the prairie, havin' spasms. The shepherd tells this good Samaritan that he's swallered strychnine.

"Now, most cowmen them days would have let a wooly herder slip across the divide with the wolf bait in him, but Bill's heart softens, an' the way he quirts his hoss down the hind leg for camp is scary. When he returns at the same gait, he's packin' a ten-pound lard can, an' buildin' a chip fire he warms this hog fat till it runs easy. Then with the help of an iron spoon an' three or four ₁ood calf-rastlers to hold him, Bill empties the whole ten pounds into the shepherd. About the time Bill runs out of lard, a stranger rides up an' breaks the news to him that he's treatin' a case of snakes from Billings booze instead of strychnine. The herder recovers, but for six months he sweats straight leaf lard, an' his hide's so slick he can hardly keep his garments on.

"There's one gentleman from Great Falls in the party who don't deal in livestock, and whose name spells strong of Irish. This gent is drinkin' coca cola, but judgin' by the expression in his eye, Teddy Blue thinks some jobber has slipped something else into his beverage. He gets so lit up one night in the sleeper that he dreams he's a dry goods store and yells fire, which causes a panic and many of the peaceful sleepers leaped from the upper berths. One heavy man—the gent from the Sun River valley—was lucky enough to fall on his head, so he wasn't injured none.

"Joe Scanlan, the Lord Northcliffe of Milestown, seems to be actin' as head of the entertainment committee, an' he must have used up a month's supply of gasoline in two days, haulin' friends and strangers to points of interest, like the Powder River special on the Milwaukee tracks.

"One of the attractions that the visitors enjoyed at Miles was Huffman's collection of range pictures at the fine art studio he has built to keep 'em in. Huffman was post photographer at Fort Keogh in the old Indian fightin' days of the '70s, and is one of the real old-timers in this business in Montana, which his pictures show.

"Teddy Blue meets an old friend of his, Jack Hawkins, who he hasn't seen for years. Hawkins is an old Texas ranger, an' he drifts into Montana as a buffalo hunter in the late '70s. He's later sheriff of Custer County. Hawkins has seen some real fightin' when Indians an' outlaws was bad in the early days in Texas. If you want to hear a good story some time, ask Jack about scalpin' a Comanche.

"Although Miles has always been a cow town, it's earned the right to be called a city, an' they handled the visitors in the old welcome way of the West."

WIDE RANGES

RANCHES

THE cow ranches that I knowed," says Rawhide Rawlins, "is nothing like them they're running to-day. In the old days, it wasn't much, only a place to winter. They were on a stream or river bottom. The buildings were made of what the country gave —logs, either cottonwood or pine in the North. They had one house —maybe two, with a shed between, a stable, and a pole corral. All these buildings were dirt roof, some had no floor but ground. There was no fences, not even a pasture. South of Colorado these buildings were adobe. Out on the treeless plains where there's no timber, they were sod.

"A few tons of wild hay were put up for a little bunch of saddle hosses for winter. This was put up, not by cowpunchers, but by some outsider that wanted work.

"Cows sound like milk, but if a cowpuncher got milk it was Eagle Brand. A cowpuncher might work a brand over or steal a slick ear, but he wouldn't steal milk from a calf.

"I never knowed but one woman on a cow ranch, and she wore moccasins an' smoked willow bark. I'm talkin' about the days of the open range when there wasn't a wire from the Arctic Sea to the Gulf of Mexico. There were no dogs, no chickens—some had a cat, but he had to rustle for his grub during the summer months. There was a cat hole in the door with a little swinging door that the cat could open, and don't think he couldn't handle it—'specially if a coyote, or his big cousin, Mr. Bob Cat, showed up. He liked to see the snow come 'cause he knowed that would drive the punchers home, and maybe you think he didn't purr when the boys came home; he was sure loving.

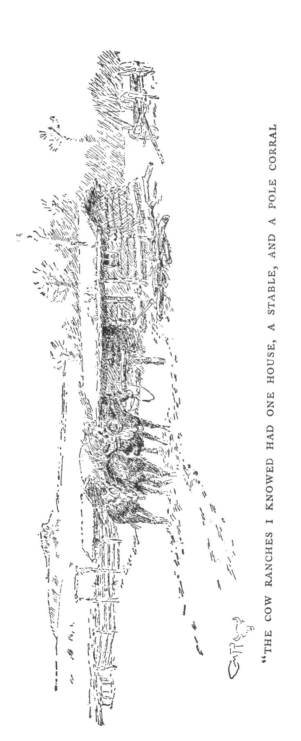

"THE COW RANCHES I KNOWED HAD ONE HOUSE, A STABLE, AND A POLE CORRAL"

"Barring line riders that were stationed at a lonesome line camp, cowpunchers put in their time at the stage station playing monty or stud poker. Most cow hands were whiskey drinkers. Some of them wintered in cow towns, either tending bar, gambling, or working in a livery stable—a cow hand could hold down any of these jobs. The booze joints he worked in, he tended bar with his hat on. He was good around hosses, and most always was a gambler. On the range he played on a blanket; in town he could generally hold his own on a round table agin tin horns. Some punchers hung around at the ranch, making hackamores and ropes. Reading matter was scarce—a saddle catalog, maybe a back number *Police Gazette*, sometimes a well-worn stray novel. In the long winter nights their light was coal-oil lamps or candles—sometimes they were forced to use a 'bitch,' which was a tin cup filled with bacon grease and a twisted rag wick. It didn't only give light—it gave its owners a smell like a New England dinner.

"When spring came, cowpunchers gathered hosses an' rode bog till the roundup time.

"Most of the cow ranches I've seen lately was like a big farm. A bungalow with all modern improvements, a big red barn that holds white-faced bulls an' hornless milk cows. The corrals are full of fancy chickens, there's a big garage filled with all kinds of cars, and at the bunkhouse that sets back where the owner and his family can't see or hear them, are the hands.

"You might see a man with a big hat, boots, and spurs—he's the fence rider—but most of them wear bib overalls. The boss wears puttees and a golf cap.

"The bungalow, that's got electric lights an' hot and cold water. There's a piana that you play with your feet, and a radio, a Mah Jong set, and a phonograph. The owner, if he's an old-timer, don't care for this. He'd rather camp in the bunkhouse and talk to some old bowleg about cows that wore horns. But maybe the woman he's tied to is the new kind. If she is, she's got paw whip-broke. She's out for sheriff. She's that kind. She's been wearin' the bell since she stepped in her loop, so paw, like any other good pack-hoss, takes anything you put on him. He's wearin' golf socks and knickerbockers and when he meets his old friends, looks ashamed.

"If they've got a son or daughter, these come home during vacation. The daughter goes to finishin' school, she's got her hair bobbed. At this school she learns to smoke, and wears less clothes and makes 'em stay on with less visible support than any since the days of Eve. If she or her brother ride at all, they ride with an English saddle an' English boots. Both her and her brother can knock a golf ball so far a bloodhound couldn't find it in a week—but there's a hired girl in the house to pass the biscuits.

"Son can play football. He's good with the gloves and can do all kinds of tricks with Injun clubs, but with an ax he's plumb harm-less. He couldn't split enough wood to cook a flapjack, in a month. He can find the button that turns on the light but he couldn't find one of his dad's calves in a corral with a bell on. Maybe he could find work, but he never looks for it.

"All these folks have been across the big water. Paw didn't care to go, but ma was wearing the bell, so he trails along—him an' his checkbook. They've traveled in the Alps with a Swiss guide, but nary one of them ever saw the Yellerstone or Glacier Park.

"The cow ranch to-day," says Rawhide, "is a place to make money to go somewheres else."

FASHIONS

IN GRANDDAD'S time, when a man starts looking for his mate, he's sure gambling. If the lady limps he might think her shoes hurt, but maybe she's got a wooden leg; with the yards of garments she's wearing, he can't tell. What she's got on would overdress a ballroom to-day. He's only got two safe bets—her face and her hands. Of course she's wearing long hair, but her head is another gamble; maybe it's got bumps like a summer squash; and maybe the hair that hides it is a wig. She'd look the same with a night-cap on in a feather bed. As I said before, "Our grandpaws was sure gamblers!"

It's different to-day. Bobbed hair, short skirts, low front and back—every rag she's wearing wouldn't pad a crutch. If you think you're getting the worst of it, take the lady to the seashore, get her wet in her one-piece suit and you don't need no X-ray—the cards are face up on the table; scars, warts, or pimples, they are all in sight —all you got to do now is find out what brand of cigarettes she uses.

I used to think that men could stand more punishment than women, but I was wrong. In winter a girl wears a fox skin, but her brisket is bared to the weather, and there ain't nothin' on her that's warmer than a straw hat. But she don't pound her feet nor swing her arms. If she's cold nobody knows it. If a man would go out dressed this way, there ain't doctors enough in the world to save him. No sir, a woman can go farther with a lipstick than a man with a Winchester and a side of bacon.

"ALL THESE RIDERS GO TO CAMP FOR DINNER"

THERE'S mighty little open range left, barring the mountains—it's all under wire now. There's countries in the Southwest where the horned toad still lives undisturbed.

Most cow countries now are pastures. The old-time roundups of the old days are almost a thing of the past. Before they strung wire, cow ranges were divided by imaginary lines. These lines were ridden by line riders who kept most of the cattle on their own ranges.

In the spring cowmen came to a set meeting place with their riders. The number of riders a cowman had was according to the size of his herd. In the Northwest, I've seen as high as a hundred men, though not often so many. I worked on roundup where there was seventy-five men with over four hundred head of saddle horses. These were handled by hoss wranglers night and day.

In the country I knowed, the first thing done in the spring by cowpunchers was to gather hosses. The roundup captain had to know all the brands and the country. When they all had met, these folks started working the country for calves. When the punchers were all saddled, the whole bunch left camp. The roundup ground was generally within a mile of camp. The captain rode out with his bunch and did what's called scatterin' his riders. As I said before, these cowboys know the range and they know where the most cows are, so the captain sends his riders according. Maybe he'll say, "Slim, you an' Bill and Frank go out to the head of Lone Injun and work them Clear Lake flats." Maybe it's twenty miles. If it's a long ride, it's called the outside circle. "Slack, you and Curley with Owens comb them dry Wolf Flats." He does this till he's sent them all on circle in different sized bunches according to the number of cattle they'd find.

The sun ain't up yet and maybe they're all back by noon, bringing lots of cows and calves. They're all thrown into one big herd. Maybe there's a thousand head. Now, all these riders, barring a few that's left to hold herd, go to camp for dinner. By the time they're through the hoss wrangler has the hosses in the rope corral. Then these punchers rope out their fast or "cut" hosses, saddle and ride to the herd. Then they ride in and cut out all cows with calves, each puncher taking out cows that's wearing the brand he's working for.

In old times when they branded on the prairie, separate herds were held to the side of the main herd—these were called "cuts." A fire was built nearby, where they kept the irons hot. These punchers roped calves from the cut and dragged them to the fire where two men afoot, called "rustlers," took them off the rope, and the "iron man" branded and ear-marked them. If the herd was too big and they couldn't brand all the calves, the unbranded calves were held with their mothers, night-herded and branded next day.

This was kept up all summer, moving camp according to how many cattle held. The fall roundup was the same, except steers and all cattle considered beef were cut out of the herd and night-herded. The last thing was trailing the beef to the railroads. In old times, these beef herds were trailed hundreds of miles to the railroads.

I'm only telling about cow countries I know—different countries handled cows different ways. In some southern countries a roundup was called a "rodeo," and cowpunchers was called "buckaroos." Most of them were known by this name west of the mountains from California to Oregon. I have heard Texas men call a roundup a "cow hunt."

BRONC TWISTERS

TALKIN' about bronc twisters," says Rawhide Rawlins, "there's some difference between hoss fighters to-day an' them I knowed years ago. I ain't sayin' these up-to-date riders ain't good as they ever was, an' I'd bet there's more of 'em than in the old days. The bronc rider always was and always will be a game glory hunter, gritty as a fish-egg rolled in sand, but the lives they live to-day an' the rigs they ride are different.

"The modern bronc fighter saddles an' steps across the bronc in a narrer chute, or he's got a bunch of hoss handlers earin' the animal down till he saddles an' mounts. Of course he's got rules to ride under, such as keepin' one hand up, keepin' his spurs loose an' scratchin'. He ain't allowed to change hands, reach for or touch nothin'. The snake he's ridin' is an old outlaw from six to fifteen years old, an' he's grain-fed. It's a cinch a hoss with a paunch full of oats is stronger than one with a grass belly.

"These modern twisters ride a swell-fork saddle with high horn. The cantle is also high an' steep. Their spurs are long and straight-shanked. This is the contest rider I'm talkin' about, an' he's a sure-enough glory rider. When he breaks away from the chute in the middle of a twistin' snake, there's thousands of folks yellin' their heads off, but more'n half of 'em's howlin' for the hoss. There's generally three judges on hosses follerin' him, seein' he don't pull nothin' crooked.

"The big half of the folks that take in ridin' contests never rode nothin' but cushions, so if Mister Buster gets unloaded, they say he couldn't ride; if he stays an' scratches his bronc they say the hoss didn't buck. But there's always a few old bowlegs that have went straight up to the end of the bridle reins who heap savvy, an' are ready to shake hands with this bronc rider whether he stays or hits the ground. These twisters of to-day are made of the same leather as the old-time ones. It ain't their fault that the country's fenced an' most of the cows are wearin' bells.

"Now the old bronc fighter I knowed, lived when there wasn't a wire from the Arctic Sea to the Gulf of Mexico, an' that whole stretch was mighty near all his home. This gent lived on either cow or hoss ranges. His saddle was a straight-fork with a cantle that sloped back, an' compared to saddles now, the horn was low. I've seen bronc riders use an old macheer saddle with a Texas tree. It had two cinches an' was called a 'rim-fire.' The horn was low an' flat—so big you couldn't more'n span it with your hand. The macheer, as it was called, was one piece of leather that fitted over the cantle an' horn, makin' a coverin' for the whole rig. This leather was smooth an' so slick it wasn't easy to stay in.

"These old-timers' spurs had crooked shanks that turned down. They all rode an' broke broncs with a hackamore. It wasn't a rope one like they're usin' to-day, but one made of braided leather an' rawhide. Looped to this was about fifteen or twenty foot of hair rope called a 'McCarthy.' This was wrapped around the lower end of the noseband under the jaws of the hoss, makin' reins an' a tie-rope.

"Range hosses them days was wild as buffalo, an' corraling a bunch wasn't always easy. But Mister Bronc Fighter's work really begun after the gate was closed or the bars up, for the first thing was to rope the one he figgered on ridin'. Generally he fore-footed him. This made him fairly safe in front, but a bronc's dangerous at both ends, an' the bronc fighter knows this. He ain't takin' chances, an' after he's got the bronc's front feet snared, he man-handles him till he gets the hackamore on. Then, sometimes usin' a blind, he saddles him an' steps across.

"Mebbe this bronc's a snake, an' mebbe he's easy, but either way there ain't nobody watchin' but the other broncs. If the bronc fighter rides him outside the corral he might buck through a bunch of range cows, but neither cows nor broncs seem to appreciate good ridin', so there's nobody boostin' for this twister. The old bronc riders didn't only ride a bronc, but they worked him. They'd take a string of rough ones to a roundup an' ride circle, cut cattle or rope off of him.

"All these things happened in the good old days long ago, when men like Con Price, Charlie Brewster, Windy Bill Davis, Kid Price, Little Jack Davis, Happy Jack Anderson, Jim Dency, Ed Rhodes, Joe Doles, Charlie Parks, Johnny Van, Bill Shaules, and Colonel Johnson were needed on all the cow ranges. These men were all well known when Montana was a cow country. They were all riders that rode smooth fork.

"Some of these old riders is friends of mine. Charlie Brewster's one of the best that ever stepped across a hoss, an' many a bad one he's tamed. One time Charlie's ridin' on a roundup. Of course his string's all broncs, an' one mornin' he'll never forget he's got a snaky roan under him an' starts out on circle with six other punchers in the Deep Creek country. This stream in places is walled in with rimrock cliffs that run up twenty to sixty feet above the bottom.

"They're ridin' along mebbe twenty yards from the edge of one of these rims, when Charlie drops his hackamore reins an' builds a cigarette. Most men ridin' a hoss like this roan would be careful, but it's different with Charlie. He don't fear no hoss on earth, an' he ain't askin' no bronc whether he objects to smokin'. While he's rollin' his smoke the roan drops his ear down an' shows the white of his eyes, so it's easy to guess his feelin's is hurt. Charlie strikes a match, but he never lights his cigarette. While he's cuppin' his hands over the match, lettin' the sulphur burn off, somethin'—

mebbe the brimfire sniff he gets—wakes the hell in the roan. He kicks the lid off, hides his head an' starts for the rimrock.

"Charlie has plenty of time to quit, but does he step off? Don't ever think it. He sinks the steel into the roan's right shoulder and throws his weight on the left rein, but he don't turn him. The roan's goin' high an' scary when he hits the edge of the cliff an' goes over.

"There's a feller called Oregon John with Brewster when he takes that long jump. Oregon tells me that when he sees Charlie sink into the landscape he's afraid to look over, but he'd have bet what he's got an' all he could beg, borrow, or steal, that at the bottom he'll find a scramble of man an' hoss meat.

"None of the bunch says nothin', but ridin' up easy, like they're goin' to a funeral, they peek over, an' what do you think they see? There, mebbe ten feet below the rimrock, sits Charlie in the middle of the roan. The bronc's lookin' healthy, but uncomfortable. He's lodged in the top of a big cottonwood. Charlie's still holdin' his cigarette, an' when the boys show up he hollers: 'Anybody got a match? The one I struck blowed out.'

"Oregon says that bronc's sure helpless, for he's wedged in the old tree so he can't more than move an ear. One of the boys goes to camp an' brings an axe, an' they have to fall the tree to get the roan out.

"This story may sound fishy to some folks, but it's true. Charlie Brewster's still in Montana, an' I'll bet wherever he is, he's still with hosses. He was a real bronc rider, an' all old-time cowmen knew him.

"I remember another old-time bronc fighter that could ride any hoss livin' an' work with him. His name's Con Price, an' right now he's with a cow outfit in California. There's a story about him that a lot of old cowmen will remember an' laugh about.

"Con's out one time with Ed Rosser, huntin' hosses. They're

"THE BRONC'S LODGED IN THE TOP OF A BIG COTTONWOOD"

riding the high country, when Rosser pulls up his hoss an' points to a nester's cabin in a little valley below. 'There's women in that shack,' says he.

"'What makes you think so?' asks Con.

"'I see washin' on the line there a few days ago,' says Rosser, 'an' all the he-folks we know, when they do any washin', use the creek an' hang their clothes on the willers. But to make my belief a cinch bet, there's garments on that line that ain't worn by no he-people.'

"'Well, I guess you're right,' Con says. 'I remember a few weeks ago that nester told me he had a wife an' daughter comin' out from the States.'

"'Wonder what the gal looks like,' says Rosser.

"'She's a good looker, judgin' from the photograph the old man shows me,' Con answers.

"In the days when this happens, women 're scarce, an' the few cowpunchers an' old mountain men that lived in this womanless land sure liked to see a white woman an' hear her voice. So Con an' Rosser start figgerin' on some kind of an excuse to visit this ranch. They can't ask for a drink of water, 'cause the hills are full of springs an' they have to cross the creek to get to the cabin.

"They're both studyin' when Con gets a plumb new one. The hoss he's ridin's a snuffy old boy. If you thumb him or hang the steel in his shoulder he'll go high. Con's idea is to start him an' then fall off.

"They're mebbe fifty yards from the house when Con throws one of his hooks in the shoulder of the old hoss, hopin' somebody's lookin' from behind a curtain to see the fall he gets. Once is enough. This animal, like many of his kind, considers this an insult, an' sinkin' his head, he starts for the clouds.

"About the third jump Con loosens. The hoss, Con tells me later, makes the play realistic. 'When he feels me goin',' he says, 'he weaves off to one side an' I hit the ground a lot harder tnan I expected.'

"Con lays like he's hurt bad. Rosser quits his hoss an' runs to his friend, an' he's got all he can do to get him on his feet.

"'You're a sure-enough actor,' Rosser whispers to Con. 'You're as heavy as a dead bear,' he says, as he part leads an' part packs him up the hill to the house. 'If it was another twenty feet I'd have to cut hand-holds in you.'

"It's a cinch that anybody not on to the play would bet Con's got all his legs broke. A sweat's broke out all over Rosser when he gently lays Con on the step an' knocks at the door.

"Con lays there, listenin' for footsteps of the ladies, but they don't come. There's no sign of life, an' the only livin' thing in sight is two hosses—Con's and Rosser's. They're driftin' mighty rapidly homeward. The one Con rode, with the reins still over his neck, is headed like he knows where he's goin'. Rosser's is follerin' close with his head to one side, so he don't step on the reins. Lookin' at these hosses, an' nobody comin' to the door, makes Con recover mighty fast, an' his groans turns to cussin'.

"In them days, when the country was wide open an' lawless, the houses had no keys, so after knockin' a few more times, they both walk in. Rosser's right; it's a woman's camp. There's curtains on the winders and flowers growin' in a tomato can that's settin' on a table where the sun hits them. From the sign, they read there's two ladies camped here an' they ain't to home. They might have got sympathy from these ladies, but they don't get none from one another. This play of theirs turns into a hoss joke, an' of course nobody laughs but the hosses.

"It's a ten-mile ride to the ranch, an' it means twice that a-foot to these spur-heeled gents, so after prospectin', they locate some bacon, real light-bread an' a dried apple pie. Finishin' their feed they wash the dishes an' start on their sorrowful journey.

"Con laughs about it now, but Rosser says he never even smiled the day he walked. Rosser says Con had no license to kick. He'd fought hosses all his life and win most of the fights. That day he throws the fight to the hoss. The hoss, bein' crooked as Con, double-crossed him."

"I HIT THE GROUND A LOT HARDER THAN I EXPECTED"

I NEVER knowed much about the Good Book," says Rawhide Rawlins, "but there's one story I've always remembered since childhood that I heer'd at Sunday school. That's the one where this sheepherder, David, hurls a rock at Goliar an' wins the fight easy. But when I growed up I kind'of doubted this yarn till it's proved to me by the real thing that size nor weepons don't always win a battle.

"One time, years ago, I'm winterin' in a little burg. I ain't mentionin' no names, as some of the parties still live, an' havin' families it might cause the offspring to underestimate the old man.

"In this camp there's a man that's got a history back of him that's sure scary. He's wearin' several notches on his gun an' has this little burg buffaloed. This gentleman's big all ways. He stands six feet four an' he'll weigh two hundred an' fifty easy. As for looks, his features is wolfish an' his brain cavity wouldn't make a drinkin' cup for a canary bird. Knowin' he's got everybody bluffed, his feelin's is mighty easy hurt, an' most of the folks keep him soothed by buyin' drinks for him. One day a stranger forgets to buy him a drink, an' the big man bends a gun over his head.

"There's a reformed preacher in this town, runnin' a stud poker game. This feller is Bible-wise and hangs the name 'Goliar' on the big man, but when he calls him that to his face the giant gets wolfy. Misunderstandin' the name, he thinks the stud dealer's callin' him a liar. The gambler, bein' a quick thinker, is mighty fast squarin' it up an' tells him the Bible story, barrin' the finish, but whisperin' to me on the side, says he wishes David would drop in.

"Goliar has things his own way all winter, when Christmas

comes along. There's fellers from line camps, an' all the cow and hoss ranches in the country rides in to celebrate. Most of 'em, knowin' Goliar's back record an' lookin' for pleasure, not trouble, are careful about startin' arguments. They're all gamblin' an' buyin' drinks. Nobody's barred, so it's pretty soft for the big feller. The whiskey they're sellin' ain't a peaceful fluid at the best, an' with his hide full of fightin' booze, he's touchy as a teased snake. He makes a tenderfoot or two dance, but he can't get no excuse to make no killin's.

"Among these range people there's a lonesome sheepherder an' his dog. He's an undersized proposition, takes plenty of whiskey but says nothin'. He loves music an' does his entertainin' with a mouth harp, but most of the time he's sleepin' off in a corner with the best friend he's got layin' at his feet.

"These people are all mighty enthusiastic celebratin' this saintly day, an' of course there's several fights pulled, but none of 'em's finished with worse than a black eye or broken nose. One gentleman, a gun packer, reaches for his weapon once, but Goliar's standin' close to his meat. He gets his own barker first an' combs this puncher's hair. Of course this finishes the fight with the spillin' of some blood, but there's no powder burnt.

"'Long about noon this little shepherd dozes off into a nap over in a corner. All this drunken hollerin' an' talkin' don't disturb his slumbers, but it seems to work on his dog's nerves, an' when the collie can't stand it no longer, he slips out, lookin' for some of his own kind that's sober. He's soon gettin' along fine with a bunch of his species, an' is sure enjoyin' himself when Goliar, who's roamin' from one joint to another, sets eyes on him. It's pickin's for this low-minded giant, an' it ain't long before he's got this poor dog turned loose with a can hangin' to him.

"The first charge the collie makes is in among the hosses that's tied to the rack, leavin' nothin' much on the pole but broken bridle reins an' hackamore ropes, an' quite a few of the celebrators are afoot. Then Mr. Dog starts for his friend an' partner, an' when he tears into this saloon, the noise he's makin' wakens the little shepherd. The dog winds up whinin' on his master's knee.

"This shepherd's face, that has always been smilin' an' happy, looks mighty warlike now, an' it wouldn't be healthy for the canner to be close to him. Seems like he's sober in a minute. While he's untyin' the can from his dog, the owner of this booze joint, who's a dog lover himself, steps over an' slippin' a forty-five into the sheepherder's hand, whispers: 'That's Goliar's work; go get him, Shep.'

"But the sheepherder, who's cryin' now, shakes his head, an' refuses the weepon, sayin' he don't need no gun to clean up that big louse. Then he leaves without even askin' for a drink, his dog slinkin' close to his heels. He's quite a way up the street when Goliar spies him an' hollers: 'Go 'round 'em, Shep! Have you got all the black ones?' Pullin' his gun, the giant starts liftin' the dirt around the shepherd's feet.

"But the herder ain't gun-shy an' don't even side-step till one of the bullets grazes the dog, who whines an' crowds his master's legs. Whirlin' 'round, the gentle shepherd reaches down, picks up a good-sized boulder an' hurls it at Goliar, catchin' him on the point of the chin. Goliar straightens up an' falls his length, an' before he can recover the herder has tore the gun loose from the giant's clutches and is workin' him over with the barrel.

"Some one wants to stop him, but the same feller that offers him the gun tells the crowd to stand back an' let Shep finish. The stud dealer, who's watched the play from the start, says: 'Goliar got his—that's sure enough David. The same as cards, history repeats—I'd 've played Goliar with a copper.'

"This Goliar is gathered up an' sent by the next stage to the hospital where he's nursed back to life. His nose is broke, the same with his right jaw, an' one of his ears has to be sewed on.

"I ain't seen Goliar for years, but the last time I met him he's wearin' scars that's a map of the battle he had with David."

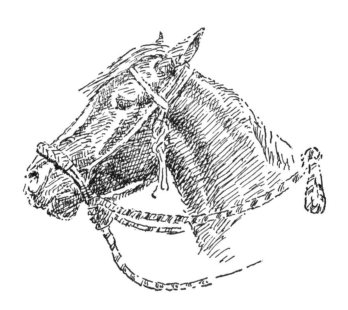

I'D BEEN over on Broken Bow, an' had seen many strange Indians in Long Pipe's camp; among 'em an old, scar-faced warrior that interested me. Knowin' Squaw Owens' acquaintance among these people, I enquire if he knows any such savage.

"From the earmarks you give me," says he, "it's old Medicine-Whip, my uncle by marriage; that Blood woman I had was his niece. When I'm a kid in Missouri I used to read yaller-back novels that was sure scary, but Medicine-Whip's history would make them romances look like a primer story. There ain't much pleasure for him since the Whites made laws agin killin' men for fun. His range is up on Belly River. I guess he's down visitin' some of his relatives, an' when an Injun goes visitin' it ain't one of them how-dye-do, how-are-you calls, where you stand awhile with your hat in your hand. It's a case of stay till the grub plays out. This social habit is one of the things that makes 'em hard to civilize; you'd as well try an' scatter a flock of blackbirds or make a bee live lonesome as to separate these people. 'Tain't their nature. In old times they bunched for protection agin their enemies, an' they've never got over likin' that way of livin'. Nature fed an' clothed her children an' taught 'em how to live, an' it'll take Uncle Sam some time to wean 'em from their mother.

"We'll say here's an Injun forty years old. He's had the dust of the runnin' herd in his nostrils, an' the clatter of dewclaws an' hoofs are still fresh in his ears, when Uncle Sam pulls him down off a high-headed, painted buffalo hoss, an' hookin' his hands around the handle of a walkin' plow, tells him it's a good thing, to push it along.

Farmin' is the hardest work on earth, an' when Uncle Sam saws off
a job like this to Mr. Injun, a gentleman that never raised nothin'
but hell an' hair, it's no wonder he backs away from the proposition.
As far back as anybody knows, his folks lived by the use of their
weapons. They sowed nothin' an' reaped nothin'. Barrin' a few
roots an' berries the women gathered, Injuns were carniverous
animals; meat was their strong holt, an' if they had that they asked
for nothin' more.

"But you were askin' about Medicine-Whip. That old savage
is the real article, an' can spin yarns of killin's an' scalpin's that
would make your hair set up like the roach on a buck antelope;
that is, if you caught him feelin' right. I ain't never got him strung
out but once.

"That's about four years ago; I'm huntin' hosses in the Ghost
Butte country. One afternoon after ridin' since sun-up with nothin'
to eat, I run on to a Blood camp an' I ain't sorry, for I'm sure
hungry. This camp's pretty quiet; barrin' a few half-naked kids
playin' an' an old squaw humped over, scrapin' a beefhide, there's
no life in sight. It's one of these hot days that makes folks hug
shadows; even the dogs, layin' in the shade of the lodges with their
tongues lollin', don't no more'n glance at me. I ask the old woman
where is the chief's lodge. She straightens up and points with her
chin to one with queer-lookin' birds painted on each side of the door.
Droppin' my reins to the ground, I slide from the saddle an' approach the gentleman's residence. Not wantin' to walk in too free,
I say 'How' when I near the door. There's an answer of 'How! How!
How!' from inside, an' stoopin' an' peekin' in, I see my old uncle.

"He's kind of half leanin' agin a willer backrest, cuttin' his
smoke mixture of red willow an' tobacco with a long butcher knife.
He never looks up from his work, but signs to me with his free hand
to come in an' sit down. Readin' his face, you wouldn't think he
knew I was there, but it's a safe bet he or some of his snake-eyed

kids had me spotted before I discovered the camp. There never
was an Injun camp without a lookout, an' when he sees anything it
don't bother him none to let the folks know. A man that can get to
an Injun camp without bein' seen has got a medal comin' for sneakin'.

"Well, after a mighty cold handshake, I sit down. He keeps
choppin' away at his tobacco with no word of welcome. While I'm
sittin' there, rollin' a smoke, he calls to a squaw outside an' tells
her somethin' I don't catch. Pretty soon the lady shows up with
some half-boiled beef an' a greasy bannock on a tin plate, along with
a cup of tea, an' sets it on the ground before me. For looks it ain't
very appetizin', but the way I'm hollered out inside, I ain't lookin'
for dainties, an' I'm not long makin' a cleanup. While I'm feedin'
I go to sizin' up Medicine-Whip. He ain't wearin' nothin' but a
clout, givin' me a chance to look him over. The lodge sides are
rolled up all around, allowin' what little breeze there is to work
under, makin' it mighty pleasant in there, while outside it's hot
enough to pop corn. An' maybe you think my uncle ain't takin'
comfort in his summer garments, while I'm clothed from heel to
chin in clothes grimed with sweat an' alkali dust; but bein' civilized,
I'm forced to stand it.

"Well, as I started to say, sizin' up this old killer, in age I'd
guess him anywhere between seventy-five an' a hundred, an' he
looks like he'll go that much more if somebody don't put his light
out. For by the scars he's wearin', he's a hard one to down, an' it's
a cinch he's packin' considerable lead under his hide right now.
His hair, that hangs loose on his shoulders, is gettin' roan; there's a
deep scar follerin' his wrinkled face from where the hair starts on his
forehead down across his left eye, windin' up at the point of his
chin. The way the bone of his cheek is caved in an' the crooked set
of his jaw, this ain't no knife wound; it's a safe bet it was a tomahawk, swung by somebody that wasn't jokin'. His thin-lipped

mouth looks like another scar under his nose; if he ever had a good feature, time, weather, an' fightin' has wiped it out. On his breast, just above the nipples, is several sets of scars. I savvy these; they're the marks of the Sun-Dance, where the skewers held him to the medicine pole, an' by the numbers, he's went through several of these sun jigs. Barrin' these, his body ain't marked up much, but his legs an' arms have sure had rough handlin'. He's a regular war map settin' up before me in his clout an' scars, but I can't read him. Knowin' Medicine-Whip to be a close-mouthed Injun, I'm wonderin' how I'll wring a story out of him. He ain't got no love for a man of my color; he hates a white man's tracks. He's fed me, but Injuns are liberal with grub, an' the chances are the beef I'm eatin' he downed on the range an' burned or buried the hide, or cut it up for moccasin soles. The Whites killed his cattle, an' he can't see where it ain't right to knock over a spotted buffalo now an' then. He'd do the same with the owner if the play came right. I don't doubt for a minute but this old uncle would down his lovin' nephew if he caught him lonesome. But even knowin' this I admire this red-handed killer. The Whites have killed his meat an' taken his country, but they've made no change in him. He's as much Injun as his ancestors that packed their quivers loaded with flint-pointed arrows, an' built fires by rubbin' sticks together. He laughs at priests an' preachers. Outside his lodge on a tripod hangs a bullhide shield an' medicine bag to keep away the ghosts. He's got a religion of his own, an' it tells him that the buffalo are comin' back. He lights his pipe, an' smokes with the sun the same as his folks did a thousand winters behind him. When he cashes in, his shadow goes prancin' off on a shadow pony, joinin' those that have gone before, to run shadow buffalo. He's seen enough of white men, an' don't want to throw in with 'em in no other world.

"Feelin' this way toward me an' my people, naturally it's hard for me to get confidential with him. He's smokin' his pipe, which he ain't never offered to me, when I break the ice of my visit by enquiring about them hosses I'm huntin'. He tells me he ain't seen or heard nothin' of 'em. Then I start fillin' him up about bein' a great warrior, an' I'd like to hear the story of them scars he's wearin'. I make this talk so smooth an' strong that he starts thawin' out, but's mighty slow loosenin' up his history. Finally, reloadin' an' lightin' his pipe, he hands it to me, an' I know he's comin' my way. Injuns are slow talkers, an' it's some time before he gathers his yarn to reel it out to me.

"On the start he straightens up, throwin' his shoulders back, an' tells me his folks was all fighters. He ain't seen three moons when his mother is killed by a Sioux war party. She's gatherin' berries, an' the Sioux try to take her prisoner, but she gets noisy an' one of the party slips a knife under her left ribs, quietin' her for always. When her folks find her, the boy's asleep, soaked in his mother's blood. The old men an' women prophesy that he will be a great warrior; it will be bad for the Sioux that meets the boy that slept in his mother's blood. An' it's the truth, 'cause before he's fifteen he downs an' scalps a Sioux, an' from that time on he makes it his business to upset an' take the hair of his enemy any time he meets one.

"He's about twenty-five when he gets these scars I'm enquirin' about. Them days this killer's known as 'Sleeps-In-Blood.' He gets the name of Medicine-Whip along with these scars. It's about this time the Crows burn the Blood range, drivin' the herd south, and his people are forced to foller up for their meat. Sleeps-In-Blood, with about fifteen warriors, is in advance of the main band. The whole camp's hungry, an' you know empty bellies don't sweeten nobody's temper. This advance guard ain't joyous; they're sure wolfy, with belts cinched to their lean flanks, an' it wouldn't be healthy for man or beast that runs into these hungry hunters. They're all rigged for war; lances, bows, an' loaded quivers. Most

"IT WOULDN'T BE HEALTHY FOR MAN OR BEAST THAT RUNS INTO THESE HUNGRY HUNTERS"

of 'em's packin' bullhide shields; a few's got smooth-bore flintlocks; their ponies're feathered an' painted.

"They're joggin' along, bad-humored, when of a sudden Sleeps-In-Blood, who's a little in advance, pulls up his pony; his bead-eye has caught a pony track in the beaten buffalo trail they're follerin'. In a minute they're all down, studyin' the tracks. As near as they can figger there's about ten ponies, an' by the way the sign's strung out, they're packin' riders.

"The sight of these tracks sets this blood-hungry bunch warlike for sure, an' they ain't slow about strippin' their saddles an' sheddin' their extra garments. Every Injun pulls his paintbag an's busy puttin' on the finishin' touches; when they're through with their toilets, they don't look like the same bunch. Sleeps-In-Blood smears his left hand with vermillion an' slaps it across his mouth, leavin' a red hand-print under his nose, showin' he's drank the enemies' blood. To keep the hair out of his eyes he wraps his foretop in weaselskin. One or two of the party's wearin' war-bonnets, but barrin' eagle or hawk feathers, the bunch ain't wearin' nothin' heavier'n paint. When everybody's striped and streaked till they look like hell's home guard, Sleeps-In-Blood lights a small warpipe, an' after a couple of whiffs holds the mouthpiece toward the sun, reelin' off a prayer that would do a preacher proud. 'See, Father, I smoke with you,' he says. 'I've lit the pipe, an' Sleeps-In-Blood does not lie when the pipe is passed. Have mercy on your children, Big Father; our parfleshes swing light at our ponies' sides; already the babies cry with empty bellies. Our enemy has burnt the grass. Now that we have struck their trail make our medicine strong!' He winds up his long, flowery prayer by handin' the pipe around to his painted brothers, who take two or three draws apiece. Then it is shaken out, an' each Injun forks his pony.

"They don't travel fast; the tracks are plain enough in the trail, but in the grass they're hard to hold. The party ain't gone far when the leaders catch sight of dust. They savvy this; it's buffalo, an' it ain't long till they hear the rumble of the runnin' herd. It's an easy guess the enemy they're follerin's among 'em, an' raisin' the next hill they sight 'em. A glimpse shows they're Sioux, so busy gettin' meat they're careless, allowin' Sleeps-In-Blood an' his men to ride up in plain sight.

"The Bloods are wise an' don't jump 'em right away, givin' 'em time to fag their ponies. Then, slippin' into the dust of the herd, they go to work on 'em an' down three before the Sioux savvy what they're up against. But, as soon as they do, they ain't slow about quittin' the herd. Now buffalo runnin' is hard on hoss flesh; they ain't gone no distance till the Sioux ponies, plumb winded, throw their tails up. They're makin' a slow runnin' fight of it when Sleeps-In-Blood kills the pony under the Sioux medicine man, causin' his party to pull up an' bunch. They're pretty well heeled, most of 'em packin' guns, an' the way they handle 'em keeps the Bloods at a respectful distance. From what old Medicine-Whip tells me, the Sioux are sure makin' a good standoff. Twice they charge 'em, an' each time a pony comes back shy a rider. These charges ain't successful; they've lost two men an' have three cripples out of the fight. The Bloods are plumb buffaloed, an' it looks like it's goin' to be a drawn battle. Sleeps-In-Blood an' his men have pulled off out of range an' are bunched up, makin' medicine, when a Sioux starts shoutin' abuse to 'em in their own tongue. This might sound strange to anyone that don't know Injuns. In those times, women were counted as plunder an' were taken as such by war parties. The speaker is either a renegade Blood or his mother a stolen woman an' she's learnt her offspring the tongue of her people. He hollers to them that it ain't no credit to a Sioux to take the hair of a Blood: these trophies are only good to trim squaw leggin's with, or make wigs for dolls for the youngsters. He said that the Sioux, when they take Bloods prisoners, don't kill 'em, but keep 'em to pack water for the squaws. Then he starts pickin' on Sleeps-In-Blood, who is sittin' on his pinto pony.

"'That pony,' said he, describin' Sleeps-In-Blood's animal, 'is a war hoss. Why is he under a woman? No,' says he, shadin' his eyes with his hand, 'it's a maggot I see. Do the Bloods allow the flies to blow their ponies' backs? Come, pony, to a warrior who will clean your back before it rots. The smell is already bad on the wind.' The Sioux all laughed long and loud.

"This talk makes Sleeps-In-Blood madder than a teased snake, an' he hollers back: 'Has the liar said all? The Sioux call themselves hunters, but they lay in camp and eat their brothers, the dog!'

"You may not know it but the Bloods are one tribe that don't eat dog, an' say it is not good to eat those who guard your camp, an' howl at your door with lonesomeness when you're gone.

"'It's a poor hunter that eats his friends,' goes on Sleeps-In-Blood. 'If the liar has more to say, let him speak fast, for in less time than it takes to smoke the warpipe, his tongue will be stilled for always; for he you call the maggot will whip your medicine man like he would a bad woman.'

"With that he throws to the ground his bow an' nearly empty quiver. He has already got his rawhide rope wrapped 'round an' 'round his pony's belly, an' by shovin' his legs under an' crampin' his knees back with feet stuck in the rope below, he's as good as tied. This is often done by Indians when chargin' a dangerous place, knowin' if they are wounded or killed the pony will pack them out. If the pony is downed, the Indian takes a chance of cuttin' himself loose with his scalpin' knife. So, as I said before, he throws down his bow and empty quiver, an' flies at them. This sure surprises the Sioux: before you could bat your eye, he's among 'em.

"The feller that has been doin' the talkin' is standin' on the edge of the bunch, an' as Sleeps-In-Blood reaches him he shoves his lance up under the Sioux's ribs, hollerin': 'If I'm a maggot I give meat to my brothers!' The lance catches in the Sioux's carcass, and Sleeps-In-Blood loses it, leavin' him nothin' but his quirt an' bullhide shield, which he holds close over his vitals an' crowds in among the ponies. The last he remembers he's lashing the medicine-man across the back an' shoulders with his quirt. He's so fightin' locoed he don't feel the arrows that are piercin' his legs an' thighs. He's got 'em pretty well scattered with his quirt, when a Sioux beefs him with his tomahawk an' he flops over.

"This game charge of his rallies an' nerves up his own men so they're right at his pony's tail when he hits the Sioux bunch, who are so busy dodgin' the swing of his quirt they're killed before they come to.

"When Sleeps-In-Blood wakes up he's sure dazed. Lookin' 'round he don't seem to savvy what's happened, till one of his friends slips a knife into his hand an' tells him to go to work. Plumb locoed with the pain of his wound, he starts butcherin'. The Sioux are all dead an' scalped but two: the medicine-man an' the one that done the talkin'. They've held them two out for him to trim.

"The blood runnin' through Sleeps-In-Blood's eyes has set him mad. He couldn't have been more fiendish if he'd broke fresh from hell. He's satisfied with the locks of the medicine-man, but the way he trims that Sioux that calls him names is sure scandalous Every cut he makes means somethin' to an Injun, an' as these people believe a man lands in the next world in the shape he leaves this one, it won't be hard, he thinks, to identify this Sioux as a liar an' thief in the happy huntin' ground.

"Reelin' off this yarn has warmed my uncle up plenty; it's brought all the savage in him to the surface, an' lookin' him over, I don't doubt his story. He's been a fighter all right, an' it's in him yet."

COLUMBUS discovers America. A feller called Ponce de Leon claims he discovered Florida. Jim Bridger finds the Great Salt Lake, but it's Pat Geyser, as he's knowed by old-timers, that locates the geyser on Geyser Creek, near the town that gets its name from it. Pat Geyser ain't this gent's right name, but I ain't tippin' nobody's hand," observed Rawhide Rawlins.

"Pat tells that one day in the early '80s he's out lookin' for cows, an' the chances are good that any he takes an interest in belong to somebody else. Pat's good hearted an' he hates to see calves wanderin' around wearin' no brand. They look so homeless that he's always willin' to stake 'em to a brand with his own iron.

"Pat's hoss is dry when he rides onto this creek an' notices a muddy pool, but as there ain't no geysers in Ireland, Pat don't savvy, he says. His hoss ain't no more'n dropped his head to drink than this here geyser busts loose, takin' Pat an' the hoss along with it. There's steam, sody water, an' a mixture of all the health resorts, in this stew that's boiled over, an' Pat claims the force of it lifts his hoss from his iron shoes.

"Pat tells that he don't know how far skyward he goes, but him an' the hoss passes an eagle on the way back.

"Now I'm goin' to say here that I've seen this geyser myself, many a time, but me nor no one else, barrin' Pat, ever see it do anything more vicious than a keg of sour dough would. It just kind of bubbles once in a while.

"Havin' heard of the Yallerstone Park, an' thinkin' he's found another one, Pat starts, a few days after, buildin' a health resort, follerin' the plans of the Mammoth Hotel, but bein' built of cottonwood logs, dry weather shrinks her a lot. I remember bein' there once, and after a few drinks of Pat Geyser's favor-ite, the measure-ments swells till this shack looks like the Brown Palace in Denver.

"For the first few years Pat don't draw a strong trade, as humans are scatterin' and the only sickness in the country is scab, the sheepmen havin' dippin' tanks for that. But in time it grows into quite a resort and rest cure for shepherds. These herders don't take much to the geyser water, barrin' the little Pat throws in as a 'chaser.'

"Tenderfeet stoppin' with Pat would often ask, 'When does this geyser turn loose?'

"Pat's always there with a comeback: 'How long will you be here?'

"'Leavin' to-morrer,' the tenderfoot might say.

"'You'll just miss it by a day.' Pat had it fixed so the visitor was always shy a day or two of seein' it.

"None of the regular patrons of the resort ever see anything that ain't brought on by liquor, but by usin' enough of the rest cure medicine the bartender passed out there, a man could see northern lights at noon time, rainbows at night, an' total eclipses of the sun any time—to say nothin' of geysers of all sizes.

"Pat was strong for the social end of life, an' he used to pull card parties for freighters to break the monotony of their trips. At these no skinner was allowed to bet any more than he had. Some knockers said Pat knew both sides of the cards, but if he ever dealt off the bottom it's when nobody's lookin'.

"One afternoon when Pat's asleep the railroad sneaks in an' moves the town. The minute Pat opens his eyes he's onto their hole-card, and gettin' the wheelbarrow, he moves his hotel over to the new location an' has his dinin' room open for supper.

"When automobiles get popular, Pat, who's always progressive an' up-to-date, buys one. The day after it's delivered, Pat asks a friend to ride over to Stanford with him. They started, an' after passin' what looks like Stanford as far as he could tell at the 80-mile gait they're goin', an' seein' they're nearin' Judith Gap, the friend asks: 'What's your hurry, Pat?'

"'I'm in no hurry,' Pat yelled, 'but I'm damned if I know how to stop the thing. We'll have to let it run down.'

"The car bein' young, it has the ways of a bronc, an' Pat almost died at the wheel with his hands numb an' locked in the spokes. The friend gives him nourishment that keeps life in him, an' 18 hours later they wind up on Greybull River in Wyoming."

"THE FORCE OF IT LIFTS PAT'S HOSS FROM HIS IRON SHOES"

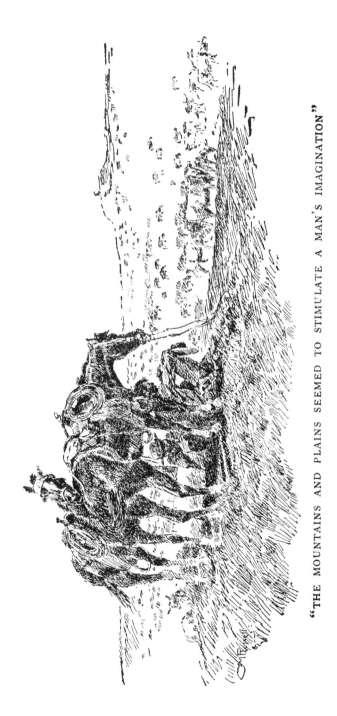

"THE MOUNTAINS AND PLAINS SEEMED TO STIMULATE A MAN'S IMAGINATION"

S PEAKIN' of liars, the Old West could put in its claim for more of 'em than any other land under the sun. The mountains and plains seemed to stimulate man's imagination. A man in the States might have been a liar in a small way, but when he comes west he soon takes lessons from the prairies, where ranges a hundred miles away seem within touchin' distance, streams run uphill and Nature appears to lie some herself.

These men weren't vicious liars. It was love of romance, lack of reading matter, and the wish to be entertainin' that makes 'em stretch facts and invent yarns. Jack McGowan, a well-known old-timer now livin' in Great Falls, tells of a man known as Lyin' Jack, who was famous from Mexico to the Arctic.

McGowan says one of Jack's favorite tales is of an elk he once killed that measured 15-feet spread between the antlers. He used to tell that he kept these horns in the loft of his cabin.

"One time I hadn't seen Jack for years," said McGowan, "when he shows up in Benton. The crowd's all glad to see Jack, an' after a round or two of drinks, asks him to tell them a yarn.

"'No, boys,' says Jack, 'I'm through. For years I've been tellin' these lies—told 'em so often I got to believin' 'em myself. That story of mine about the elk with the 15-foot horns is what cured me. I told about that elk so often that I knowed the place I killed it. One night I lit a candle and crawled up in the loft to view the horns—an' I'm damned if they was there.'"

Once up in Yogo, Bill Cameron pointed out Old Man Babcock an' another old-timer, Patrick, sayin', "there's three of the biggest liars in the world."

"Who's the third?" inquired a bystander.

"Patrick's one, an' old Bab's the other two," says Cameron.

This Babcock one night is telling about getting jumped by 50 hostile Sioux, a war party, that's giving him a close run. The bullets an' arrows are tearin' the dirt all around, when he hits the mouth of a deep canyon. He thinks he's safe, but after ridin' up it a way, discovers it's a box gulch, with walls straight up from 600 to 1,000 feet. His only get-away's where he come in, an' the Indians are already whippin' their ponies into it.

Right here old Bab rares back in his chair, closes his eyes, an' starts fondlin' his whiskers. This seems to be the end of the story, when one of the listeners asks:

"What happened then?"

Old Bab, with his eyes still closed, takin' a fresh chew, whispered: "They killed me, b' God!"

The upper Missouri River steamboats, they used to say, would run on a light dew, an' certainly they used to get by where there was mighty little water. X. Beidler an' his friend, Major Reed, are traveling by boat to Fort Benton. One night they drink more than they should. X. is awakened in the morning by the cries of Reed. On entering his stateroom, X. finds Reed begging for water, as he's dying of thirst.

X. steps to the bedside, and takin' his friend's hand, says: "I'm sorry, Major, I can't do anything for you. That damned pilot got drunk, too, last night, and we're eight miles up a dry coulee!"

"Some say rattlers ain't pizen," said Buckskin Williams, an old freighter, "but I know different. I'm pullin' out of Milk River one day with 14, when I notice my line hoss swing out an' every hoss on the near side crowds the chain. My near wheel hoss, that I'm ridin', rares up an' straddles the tongue. It's then I see what the trouble is—a big rattler has struck, misses my hoss an' hits the tongue. The tongue starts to swell up. I have to chop it off to save the wagon, an' I'm damn quick doin' it, too!"

"Cap" Nelse, a well-known old-timer around Benton in the early days, tells of coming south from Edmonton with a string of half-breed carts. They were traveling through big herds of buffalo. It was spring and there were many calves. They had no trouble with the full-grown buffalo, Cap said, but were forced to stop often to take the calves from between the spokes of the cart-wheels!

A traveling man in White Sulphur Springs makes a bet of drinks for the town with Coates, a saloon keeper, that Coates can't find a man that will hold up his hand and take his oath that he has seen 100,000 buffalo at one sight. When the bet's decided, it's agreed to ring the triangle at the hotel, which will call the town to their drinks.

Many old-timers said they had seen that many buffalo, but refused to swear to it, and it looked like Coates would lose his bet until Milt Crowthers showed up. Then a smile of confidence spread over Coates' face as he introduces Crowthers to the drummer.

"Mr. Crowthers," said the traveling man, "how many antelope have you seen at one time?"

Crowthers straightens up and looks wise, like he's turning back over the pages of the past. "Two hundred thousand," says he.

"How many elk?" asks the traveling man.

"Somethin' over a million," replies Crowthers.

"Mr. Crowthers, how many buffalo will you hold up your hand and swear you have seen at one sight?"

Crowthers holds up his hand.   "As near as I can figure," says he, "about three million billion."

This is where Coates starts for the triangle, but the traveling man halts him, saying, "Where were you when you saw these buffalo, Mr. Crowthers?"

"I was a boy travelin' with a wagon train," replies Crowthers. "We was south of the Platte when we was forced to corral our wagons to keep our stock from bein' stampeded by buffalo. For five days an' nights 50 men kep' their guns hot killin' buffalo to keep 'em off the wagons. The sixth day the herd spread, givin' us time to yoke up an' cross the Platte, an' it's a damn good thing we did."

"Why?" asks the traveling man.

"Well," says Crowthers, "we no more than hit the high country north of the Platte, than lookin' back, here comes the main herd!"

WHEN I first knowed Highwood Hank he's a cowpuncher and is pretty handy among broncs," says Rawhide Rawlins. "In them days he's ridin' for the P, and anybody that savvies that iron knows they never owned a hoss that wasn't a snake. A man had to be a rider to work for 'em. If a hoss thief found a P hoss in his bunch at daybreak, it's a cinch he'd turn him loose. P hosses was notorious.

"Kid Russell tells me he rode one summer for Ben Phillips, who owned that brand. He claimed he didn't take on no flesh that year. When he quit, his fingernails was all wore off an' there wasn't a hoss in his string that had any mane from his ears to his withers. There was spur tracks all over his saddle. He couldn't eat supper thinkin' of the hoss he had to fork the next mornin', and he never made no try at breakfast. His hands is so shaky, all that spring, that he has to get a friend to roll his cigarettes, an' if he'd worked a whole season his fingers would be wore down to the knuckles. As it is, it takes a solid year to get the crooks out of his hands from havin' 'em clamped 'round the saddle horn.

"As I said before, Hank's a rider, but like all others, old Daddy Time has hung it on him. It seems these days like his backbone has growed together in places an' it don't take to the swing of a pitchin' bronc. Hank's married now, and he's a granddad. He still owns a ranch and rides, but they ain't the long circles he used to make.

"A couple of years ago Hank runs in a bunch of broncos. They're rollin' fat an' pretty snuffy. He drops his rope on to one, an' the minute his loop tightens, Mr. Bronc swings 'round, comin' at Hank with his ears up, whistlin' like a bull elk. In the old days

"HANK'S SITTIN' ON THE GROUND WITH TWO HANDS FULL OF
CORRAL DUST"

this would a-been music to Hank's ears. It takes him back to the P string.

"Mrs. Hank's lookin' through the corral fence, an' begs Hubby not to crawl this one. He tells her not to worry.

"'All you got to do is sit back an' watch me scratch his shoulders,' he says. 'You won't have to pay no railroad fare to Miles City to see bronc ridin',' he tells her. 'This is goin' to be home talent.'

"'He'll throw you,' says she.

"'Yes, he will,' says Hank, as he cinches his hull on.

"This bronc's got his near ear dropped down an' about half of his eye shows white. He's humped till you could throw a dog under the saddle skirts behind. Hank's whistlin' 'Turkey in the Straw' to keep his sand up, an' his wife notices there's a tremble in his hand as he reaches for the horn.

"The minute the bronc feels weight on the near stirrup he starts for the clouds, an' the second time he comes down Hank ain't with him. He's sittin' on the ground with two hands full of corral dust.

"'I told you so,' says Wifie.

"'Yes, you did,' says Hank. 'You're a fine partner, sittin' there like you're deaf and dumb. Any time I ever rode a bronc before, there's always been somebody around to tell me to stay with him— to hang an' rattle. You didn't give me any encouragement. Just lookin' at you scared me loose.'

"'All right,' says Mrs. Hank, 'I'll try to do better next time.'

"But the next one is a shorter ride than the first. His better half yells: 'Stay with him!' but it's just as Hank hits the ground.

"'I hollered that time,' says she.

"'Yes, you did,' says Hank. 'Why didn't you wait till New Year's?'

"Hank hates to do it, but he has to own up that his bronc ridin' days is over."

A RACE FOR THE WAGONS

WHOEVER told you that cattle stampede without cause was talkin' like a shorthorn," says Rawhide Rawlins. "You can bet all you got that whenever cattle run, there's a reason for it. A whole lot of times cattle run, an' nobody knows why but the cows an' they won't tell.

"There's plenty of humans call it instinct when an animal does something they don't savvy. I don't know what it is myself, but I've seen the time when I'd like to a-had some. I've knowed of hosses bein' trailed a thousand miles an' turned loose, that pulled back for their home range, not goin' the trail they come, but takin' cut-offs across mountain ranges that would puzzle a bighorn. An' if you'd ask one of these wise boys how they done it, he'd back out of it easy by sayin' it's instinct. You'll find cow ponies that knows more about the business than the men that rides 'em.

"There's plenty of causes for a stampede; sometimes it's a green hand or a careless cowpuncher scratchin' a match to light a cigarette. Maybe it's something on the wind, or a tired night-hoss spraddles and shakes himself, an' the poppin' of the saddle leather causes them to jump the bed-ground. Scare a herd on the start, and you're liable to have hell with them all the way. I've seen bunches well trail-broke that you couldn't fog off the bed-ground with a slicker an' six-shooter; others, again, that had had a scare, you'd have to ride a hundred yards away from to spit. Some men's too careful with their herd an' go tiptoein' around like a mother with a sick kid. I've had some experience, an' claim this won't do. Break 'em so they'll stand noise; get 'em used to seein' a man afoot, an' you'll have less trouble.

"There's some herds that you dassen't quit your hoss short of five hundred yards of. Of course it's natural enough for cow-brutes that never see hoss an' man apart to scare some when they see 'em separate. They think the top of this animal's busted off, an' when they see the piece go movin' around they're plenty surprised; but as I said before, there's many reasons for stampedes unknown to man. I've seen herds start in broad daylight with no cause that anybody knows of. The smell of blood will start 'em goin'; this generally comes off in the mornin' when they're quittin' the bed-ground. Now, in every herd you'll find steers that's regular old rounders. They won't go to bed like decent folks, but put in the night perusin' around, disturbin' the peace. If there's any bulls in the bunch, there's liable to be fightin'. I've often watched an old bull walkin' around through the herd an' talkin' fight, hangin' up his bluff, with a bunch of these rounders at his heels. They're sure backin' him up—boostin' an' ribbin' up trouble, an' if there's a fight pulled off you should hear these trouble-builders takin' sides; every one of 'em with his tongue out an' his tail kinked, buckin' an' bellerin, like his money's all up. These night ramblers that won't go to bed at decent hours, after raisin' hell all night, are ready to bed down an' are sleepin like drunks when decent cattle are walkin' off the bed-ground.

"Now, you know, when a cow-brute quits his bed he bows his neck, gaps an' stretches all the same as a human after a night's rest. Maybe he accidentally tromps on one of these rounders' tails that's layin' along the ground. This hurts plenty, and Mr. Night Rambler ain't slow about wakin' up; he raises like he's overslept an' 's afeared he'll miss the coach, leavin' the tossel of his tail under the other fellow's hoof. He goes off wringin' his stub an' scatterin' blood on his rump an' quarters. Now the minute them other cattle winds the blood, the ball opens. Every hoof's at his heels barkin' and bellerin'. Them that's close enough are hornin' him in the flank like they'd stuck to finish him off. They're all plumb hog-wild, an' if you want any beef left in your herd you'd better cut out the one that's causin' the excitement, 'cause an hour of this will take off more taller than they'll put on in a month.

"Cattle like open country to sleep in. I sure hate to hold a herd near any brakes or deep 'royos, 'cause no matter how gentle a herd is, let a coyote or any other animal loom up of a sudden close to 'em an' they don't stop to take a second look, but are gone like a flash in the pan. Old bulls comin' up without talkin' sometimes jump a herd this way, an' it pays a cowpuncher to sing when he's comin' up out of a 'royo close to the bed-ground.

"Some folks'll tell you that cowboys sing their cows to sleep, but that's a mistake, judgin' from my experience, an' I've had some. The songs an' voices I've heard around cattle ain't soothin'. A cowpuncher sings to keep himself company; it ain't that he's got any motherly love for these longhorns he's put to bed an' 's ridin' herd on; he's amusin' himself an' nobody else. These ditties are generally shy on melody an' strong on noise. Put a man alone in the dark, an' if his conscious is clear an' he ain't hidin' he'll sing an' don't need to be a born vocalist. Of course singin's a good thing around a herd, an' all punchers know it. In the darkness it lets the cows know where you're at. If you ever woke up in the darkness an' found somebody—you didn't know who or what—loomin' up over you, it would startle you, but if this somebody is singin' or whistlin', it wouldn't scare you none. It's the same with Mr. Steer; that snaky, noiseless glidin' up on him's what scares the animal.

"All herds has some of these lonesomes that won't lie down with the other cattle, but beds down alone maybe twenty-five to thirty yards from the edge of the herd. He's got his own reason for this; might be he's short an eye. This bein' the case you can lay all you got he's layin' with the good blinker next to the herd. He don't figure on lettin' none of his playful brothers beef his ribs from a sneak. One-eyed hoss is the same. Day or night you'll find him on the outside with his good eye watchin' the bunch. Like Mister Steer, the confidence he's got in his brother's mighty frail.

"But these lonesome cattle I started to tell you about, is the ones that a puncher's most liable to run onto in the dark, layin' out that way from the herd. If you ride onto him singin', it don't startle Mr. Steer; he raises easy, holdin' his ground till you pass; then he lays down in the same place. He's got the ground warm an' hates to quit her. Cows, the same as humans, like warm beds. Many's the time in cool weather I've seen some evil-minded, low-down steer stand around like he ain't goin' to bed, but all the time he's got his eye on some poor, undersized brother layin' near by, all innocent. As soon as he thinks the ground's warm he walks over, horns him out an' jumps his claim. This low-down trick is some-times practiced by punchers when they got a gentle herd. It don't hurt a cowpuncher's conscience none to sleep in a bed he stole from a steer.

"If you ride sneakin' an' noiseless onto one of these lonesome fellers, he gets right to his feet with dew-claws an' hoofs rattlin', an' 's runnin' before he's half up, hittin' the herd like a canned dog, an' quicker than you can bat an eye the whole herd's gone. Cows are slow animals, but scare 'em an' they're fast enough; a thousand will get to their feet as quick as one. It's sure a puzzler to cowmen to know how a herd will all scare at once, an' every animal will get on his feet at the same time. I've seen herds do what a cowpuncher would call 'jump'—that is, to raise an' not run. I've been lookin' across a herd in bright moonlight—a thousand head or more, all down; with no known cause there's a short, quick rumble, an' every hoof's standin'.

"I've read of stampedes that were sure dangerous an' scary, where a herd would run through a camp, upsettin' wagons an' trompin' sleepin' cowpunchers to death. When day broke they'd be fifty or a hundred miles from where they started, leavin' a trail strewn with blood, dead cowpunchers, an' hosses, that looked like the work of a Kansas cyclone. This is all right in books, but the feller that writes 'em is romancin' an' don't savvy the cow. Most stampedes is noisy, but harmless to anybody but the cattle. A herd in a bad storm might drift thirty miles in a night, but the worst run I ever see, we ain't four miles from the bed-ground when the day broke.

"This was down in Kansas; we're trailin' beef an' have got about seventeen hundred head. Barrin' a few dry ones the herd's straight steers, mostly Spanish longhorns from down on the Cimarron. We're about fifty miles south of Dodge. Our herd's well broke an' lookin' fine, an' the cowpunchers all good-natured, thinkin' of the good time comin' in Dodge.

"That evenin' when we're ropin' our hosses for night guard, the trail boss, 'Old Spanish' we call him—he ain't no real Spaniard, but he's rode some in Old Mexico an' can talk some Spanish—says to me: 'Them cattle ought to hold well; they ain't been off water four hours, an' we grazed 'em plumb onto the bed-ground. Every hoof of 'em's got a paunch full of grass an' water, an' that's what makes cattle lay good.'

"Me an' a feller called Longrope's on first guard. He's a center-fire or single-cinch man from California; packs a sixty-foot rawhide riata, an' when he takes her down an' runs about half of her into a loop she looks big, but when it reaches the animal, comes pretty near fittin' hoof or horn. I never went much on these long-rope boys, but this man comes as near puttin' his loop where he wants as any l ever see. You know Texas men ain't got much love for a single rig, an' many's the argument me an' Longrope has on this subject. He claims a center-fire is the only saddle, but I 'low that they'll do all right on a shad-bellied western hoss, but for Spanish pot-gutted ponies they're no good. You're ridin' up on his withers all the time.

"When we reach the bed-ground most of the cattle's already down, lookin' comfortable. They're bedded in open country, an' things look good for an easy night. It's been mighty hot all day, but there's a little breeze now makin' it right pleasant; but down the west I notice some nasty-lookin' clouds hangin' 'round the new moon that's got one horn hooked over the skyline. The storm's so far off that you can just hear her rumble, but she's walkin' up on us slow, an' I'm hopin' she'll go 'round. The cattle's all layin' quiet an' nice, so me an' Longrope stop to talk awhile.

"'They're layin' quiet,' says I.

"'Too damn quiet,' says he. 'I like cows to lay still all right, but I want some of the natural noises that goes with a herd this size. I want to hear 'em blowin' off, an' the creakin' of their joints, showin' they're easin' themselves in their beds. Listen, an' if you hear anything I'll eat that rimfire saddle of yours—grass rope an' all.'

"I didn't notice till then, but when I straighten my ears it's quiet as a grave. An' if it ain't for the lightnin' showin' the herd once in a while, I couldn't a-believed that seventeen hundred head of longhorns lay within forty feet of where I'm sittin' on my hoss. It's gettin' darker every minute, an' if it wasn't for Longrope's slicker I couldn't a-made him out, though he's so close I could have touched him with my hand. Finally it darkens up so I can't see him at all. It's black as a nigger's pocket; you couldn't find your nose with both hands.

"I remember askin' Longrope the time.

"'I guess I'll have to get help to find the timepiece,' says he, but gets her after feelin' over himself, an' holdin' her under his cigarette takes a long draw, lightin' up her face.

"'Half-past nine,' says he.

"'Half an hour more,' I says. 'Are you goin' to wake up the next guard, or did you leave it to the hoss-wrangler?'

"'There won't be but one guard to-night,' he answers,'an' we'll ride it. You might as well hunt for a hoss thief in heaven as look for that camp. Well, I guess I'll mosey 'round.' An' with that he quits me.

"The lightnin' s playin' every little while. It ain't making much noise, but lights up enough to show where you're at. There ain't no use ridin'; by the flashes I can see that every head's down. For a second it'll be like broad day, then darker than the dungeons of hell, an' I notice the little fire-balls on my hoss's ears; when I spit there's a streak in the air like strikin' a wet match. These little fire-balls is all I can see of my hoss, an' they tell me he's listenin' all ways; his ears are never still.

"I tell you, there's something mighty ghostly about sittin' up on a hoss you can't see, with them two little blue sparks out in front of you wigglin' an' movin' like a pair of spook eyes, an' it shows me the old night hoss is usin' his listeners pretty plenty. I got my ears cocked, too, hearing nothin' but Longrope's singin'; he's easy three hundred yards across the herd from me, but I can hear every word:

"*Sam Bass was born in Injiana,*
It was his native home,
'Twas at the age of seventeen
Young Sam began to roam.
He first went out to Texas,
A cowboy for to be;
A better hearted feller
You'd seldom ever see.

"It's so plain it sounds like he's singin' in my ear; I can even hear the click-clack of his spur chains against his stirrups when he moves 'round. An' the cricket in his bit—he's usin' one of them hollow conchoed half-breeds—she comes plain to me in the still-ness. Once there's a steer layin' on the edge of the herd starts snif-fin'. He's takin' long draws of the air, he's nosin' for something. I don't like this, it's a bad sign; it shows he's layin' for trouble, an' all he needs is some little excuse.

"Now every steer, when he beds down, holds his breath for a few seconds, then blows off; that noise is all right an' shows he's settlin' himself for comfort. But when he curls his nose an' makes them long draws it's a sign he's sniffin' for something, an' if any-thing crosses his wind that he don't like there's liable to be trouble. I've seen dry trail herds mighty thirsty, layin' good till a breeze springs off the water, maybe ten miles away; they start sniffin', an' the minute they get the wind you could comb Texas an' wouldn't have enough punchers to turn 'em till they wet their feet an' fill their paunches.

"I get tired sittin' there starin' at nothin', so start ridin' 'round. Now it's sure dark when animals can't see, but I tell you by the way my hoss moves he's feelin' his way. I don't blame him none; it's like lookin' in a black pot. Sky an' ground all the same, an' I ain't gone twenty-five yards till I hear cattle gettin' up around me; I'm in the herd an' it's luck I'm singing an' they don't get scared. Pullin' to the left I work cautious an' easy till I'm clear of the bunch. Ridin's useless, so I flop my weight over on one stirrup an' go on singin'.

"The lightin' 's quit now, an' she's darker than ever; the breeze has died down an' it's hotter than the hubs of hell. Above my voice I can hear Longrope. He's singin' the 'Texas Ranger' now; the Ranger's a long song an' there's few punchers that knows it all, but Longrope's sprung a lot of new verses on me an' I'm interested.

Seems like he's on about the twenty-fifth verse, an' there's danger of his chokin' down, when there's a whisperin' in the grass behind me; it's a breeze sneakin' up. It flaps the tail of my slicker an' goes by; in another second she hits the herd. The ground shakes, an' they're all runnin'. My hoss takes the scare with 'em an' 's bustin' a hole in the darkness when he throws both front feet in a badger hole, goin' to his knees an' plowin' his nose in the dirt. But he's a good night hoss an' 's hard to keep down. The minute he gets his feet under him he raises, runnin' like a scared wolf. Hearin' the roar behind him he don't care to mix with them locoed longhorns. I got my head turned over my shoulder listenin', tryin' to make out which way they're goin', when there's a flash of lightnin' busts a hole in the sky—it's one of these kind that puts the fear of God in a man, thunder an' all together. My hoss whirls an' stops in his tracks, spraddlin' out an' squattin' like he's hit, an' I can feel his heart beatin' agin my leg, while mine's poundin' my ribs like it'll bust through. We're both plenty scared.

"This flash lights up the whole country, givin' me a glimpse of the herd runnin' a little to my left. Big drops of rain are pounding on my hat. The storm has broke now for sure, with the lightnin' bombardin' us at every jump. Once a flash shows me Longrope, ghostly in his wet slicker. He's so close to me that I could hit him with my quirt an' I hollers to him, 'This is hell.'

"'Yes,' he yells back above the roar; 'I wonder what damned fool kicked the lid off.'

'I can tell by the noise that they're runnin' straight; there ain't no clickin' of horns. It's a kind of hummin' noise like a buzz-saw, only a thousand times louder. There's no use in tryin' to turn 'em in this darkness, so I'm ridin' wide—just herdin' by ear an' follerin' the noise. Pretty soon my ears tell me they're crowdin' an' comin' together; the next flash shows 'em all millin', with heads jammed together an' horns locked; some's rared up ridin' others, an' these is squirmin' like bristled snakes. In the same light I see Longrope, an' from the blink I get of him he's among 'em or too close for safety, an' in the dark I thought I saw a gun flash three times with no report. But with the noise these longhorns are makin' now, I doubt if I could a-heard a six-gun bark if I pulled the trigger myself, an' the next thing I know me an' my hoss goes over a bank, lightin' safe. I guess it ain't over four feet, but it seems like fifty in the darkness, an' if it hadn't been for my chin-string I'd a-went from under my hat. Again the light shows me we're in a 'royo with the cattle comin' over the edge, wigglin' an' squirmin' like army worms.

"It's a case of all night riding. Sometimes they'll mill an' quiet down, then start trottin' an' break into a run. Not till day-break do they stop, an' maybe you think old day ain't welcome. My hoss is sure leg-weary, an' I ain't so rollicky myself. When she gets light enough I begin lookin' for Longrope, with nary a sign of him; an' the herd, you wouldn't know they were the same cattle—smeared with mud an' ga'nt as greyhounds; some of 'em with their tongues still lollin' out from their night's run. But sizin' up the bunch, I guess I got 'em all. I'm kind of worried about Long-rope. It's a cinch that wherever he is he's afoot, an' chances is he's layin' on the prairie with a broken leg.

"The cattle's spread out, an' they begin feedin'. There ain't much chance of losin' 'em, now it's broad daylight, so I ride up on a raise to take a look at the back trail. While I'm up there viewin' the country, my eyes run onto somethin' a mile back in a draw. I can't make it out, but get curious, so spurrin' my tired hoss into a lope I take the back trail. 'Tain't no trouble to foller in the mud; it's plain as plowed ground. I ain't rode three hundred yard till the country raises a little an' shows me this thing's a hoss, an' by he white streak on his flank I heap savvy it's Peon—that's the hoss

Longrope's ridin'. When I get close he whinners pitiful like; he's lookin' for sympathy, an' I notice, when he turns to face me, his right foreleg's broke. He's sure a sorry sight with that fancy, full-stamped center-fire saddle hangin' under his belly in the mud. While I'm lookin' him over, my hoss cocks his ears to the right, snortin' low. This scares me—I'm afeared to look. Somethin' tells me I won't see Longrope, only part of him—that part that stays here on earth when the man's gone. Bracin' up, I foller my hoss's ears, an' there in the holler of the 'royo is a patch of yeller; it's part of a slicker. I spur up to get a better look over the bank, an' there tromped in the mud is all there is left of Longrope. Pullin' my gun I empty her in the air. This brings the boys that are follerin' on the trail from the bed-ground. Nobody'd had to tell 'em we'd had hell, so they come in full force, every man but the cook an' hoss-wrangler.

"Nobody feels like talkin'. It don't matter how rough men are—I've known 'em that never spoke without cussin', that claimed to fear neither God, man, nor devil—but let death visit camp an' it puts 'em thinkin'. They generally take their hats off to this old boy that comes everywhere an' any time. He's always ready to pilot you—willin' or not—over the long dark trail that folks don't care to travel. He's never welcome, but you've got to respect him.

"'It's tough—damned tough,' says Spanish, raisin' poor Longrope's head an' wipin the mud from his face with his neck-handkerchief, tender, like he's feared he'll hurt him. We find his hat tromped in the mud not fur from where he's layin'. His scabbard's empty, an' we never do locate his gun.

"That afternoon when we're countin' out the herd to see if we're short any, we find a steer with a broken shoulder an' another with a hole plumb through his nose. Both these is gun wounds; this accounts for them flashes I see in the night. It looks like, when

Longrope gets mixed in the mill, he tries to gun his way out, but the cattle crowd him to the bank an' he goes over. The chances are he was dragged from his hoss in a tangle of horns.

"Some's for takin' him to Dodge an' gettin' a box made for him, but Old Spanish says: 'Boys, Longrope is a prairie man, an' if she was a little rough at times, she's been a good foster mother. She cared for him while he's awake, let her nurse him in his sleep.' So we wrapped him in his blankets, an' put him to bed.

"It's been twenty years or more since we tucked him in with the end-gate of the bed-wagon for a headstone, which the cattle have long since rubbed down, leavin' the spot unmarked. It sounds lonesome, but he ain't alone, 'cause these old prairies has cradled many of his kind in their long sleep."